13

ECONOMIC ISSUES, PROBLEMS AND PERSPECTIVES

TAX DEDUCTIONS

ANALYSES AND PROPOSALS ON ITEMIZED AND INDIVIDUAL BASES

ECONOMIC ISSUES, PROBLEMS AND PERSPECTIVES

Additional books in this series can be found on Nova's website under the Series tab.

Additional E-books in this series can be found on Nova's website under the E-book tab.

ECONOMIC ISSUES, PROBLEMS AND PERSPECTIVES

TAX DEDUCTIONS

ANALYSES AND PROPOSALS ON ITEMIZED AND INDIVIDUAL BASES

PIERRE THIBAULT
EDITOR

NOVINKA

New York

For permission to use material from this book please contact us:
Telephone 631-231-7269; Fax 631-231-8175
Web Site: http://www.novapublishers.com

Library of Congress Cataloging-in-Publication Data

ISBN: 978-1-62808-491-7

Published by Nova Science Publishers, Inc. † New York

CONTENTS

Preface		**vii**
Chapter 1	Restrictions on Itemized Tax Deductions: Policy Options and Analysis *Jane G. Gravelle and Sean Lowry*	**1**
Chapter 2	Itemized Tax Deductions for Individuals: Data Analysis *Sean Lowry*	**61**
Chapter 3	Tax Deductions for Individuals: A Summary *Sean Lowry*	**77**
Index		**101**

PREFACE

The President and leading Members of Congress have indicated that income tax reform is a major policy objective. Some itemized deductions are visible candidates for "broadening the base" of the individual income tax and cutting back on tax expenditures and primarily consist of deductions for mortgage interest, state, and local taxes, and charitable contributions. The benefits of itemized deductions are concentrated among higher-income individuals, and that is particularly the case for state and local income tax deductions and charitable deductions. Proposals for addressing these provisions fall into two general classes. One approach could include repealing or restricting all itemized deductions. A different approach would consider each type of deduction and tailor a reform to the particular objectives and merits of the deductions, such as a lower ceiling on home mortgage interest deduction and a floor for charitable contributions. This book analyzes various proposals to restrict itemized deductions, both across-the-board and individually tailored, using standard economic criteria of economic efficiency, distribution, simplicity, and estimated revenue effects.

Chapter 1 - The President and leading Members of Congress have indicated that income tax reform is a major policy objective. Some itemized deductions are visible candidates for "broadening the base" of the individual income tax and cutting back on tax expenditures and primarily consist of deductions for mortgage interest, state and local taxes, and charitable contributions. The benefits of itemized deductions are concentrated among higher-income individuals, and that is particularly the case for state and local income tax deductions and charitable deductions.

Proposals for addressing these provisions fall into two general classes. One approach could include repealing or restricting all itemized deductions. A different approach would consider each type of deduction and tailor a reform to the particular objectives and merits of the deductions, such as a lower ceiling on home mortgage interest deduction and a floor for charitable contributions.

This report analyzes various proposals to restrict itemized deductions—both across-the-board and individually tailored—using standard economic criteria of economic efficiency, distribution, simplicity, and estimated revenue effects. In particular, this report estimates each proposal's potential to contribute to revenue-neutral reductions in income tax rates and the consequences for economic behavior.

Regardless of the class of reform undertaken, for a given revenue target, tax reform involves a trade-off between a broader base and lower income tax rates. One objective of lower rates is presumably to reduce the distortionary effects on labor supply and saving. The analysis in this report, however, shows that this trade off, with respect to effects on labor supply or saving, may be more apparent than real. Economic theory indicates that the tax rate that should determine the supply responses is not the statutory marginal tax rate but the *effective marginal tax rate* (EMTR). If part of the earnings of the last dollar is spent on tax exempt uses, then EMTRs are lower, and eliminating these deductions raises them.

It is possible for a revenue-neutral tax reform to have no effect on EMTRs, or even raise them, which, for some, may defeat the purpose of tax reform. Analysis in this report suggests that eliminating itemized deductions would increase the top EMTR by approximately 41/2 percentage points but permit a statutory rate reduction in a distributionally and revenue-neutral change by about 5 percentage points. Thus, the net effect of this change is a reduction of 1/2 a percentage point (a tenth the size of the statutory reduction). Proposals with ceilings could easily raise EMTRs.

A traditional concern of tax expenditures is generally that they distort economic behavior. However, for each type of deduction there are also some justifications, although the magnitude may be in question. The provision that may have the most support from an economic efficiency standpoint is the deduction for charitable contributions.

Some types of tax reform may simplify the tax code, but others can make it more complex. In addition, transitional rules may be needed for the mortgage interest deduction to limit the impact on taxpayers with large mortgages and to soften the potential impact on the housing market.

Chapter 2 – Reforming or limiting itemized tax deductions for individuals has gained the interest of policymakers as one way to increase federal tax revenue, increase the share of taxes paid by higher-income tax filers, simplify the tax code, or reduce incentives that might lead to inefficient economic behavior. However, limits on deductions, in the views of some, would cause adverse economic effects or changes in the distributional burden of the federal income tax code. This report is intended to identify who claims itemized deductions, for how much, and for which provisions?

This report analyzes data to inform the policy debate about reforming itemized tax deductions for individuals. In 2010, 33% of all tax filers chose to itemize their deductions rather than claim the standard deduction. In addition, the data indicate that both the share of tax filers that itemize their deductions and the amount claimed by each tax filer as adjusted gross income (AGI) increases. AGI is the basic measure of income under the federal income tax and is the income measurement before itemized deductions and personal exemptions are taken into account. Although higher-income tax filers are more likely to itemize their deductions and claim a larger amount of itemized deductions than lower-income tax filers, the majority (65.8%) of itemizers in 2010 was composed of tax filers with an AGI less than $100,000, and 91.3% of itemizers had an AGI below $200,000.

Tax filers in different income ranges tend to claim different itemized deductions. In 2010, tax filers in higher income ranges claimed deductions for charitable gifts, state and local taxes, and real estate property taxes at higher rates than tax filers in lower income ranges. For example, the deduction for charitable gifts was claimed by 46% of tax filers with an AGI between $50,000 and $100,000, whereas it was claimed by 76% to 94% of tax filers with an AGI above $100,000. Deductions for state and local taxes and the deduction for charitable gifts comprise a larger share of itemized deductions as income rises.

The four largest itemized deductions are estimated to account for 17.8% ($195.7 billion) of the approximately $1.1 trillion in tax expenditures in FY2014. These deductions are for home mortgage interest, state and local taxes, charitable gifts, and real estate taxes.

These findings have several implications for policy options that would seek to reform or limit itemized tax deductions. First, efforts to target limits on itemized tax deductions toward higher-income tax filers are limited in the amount of revenue that can possibly be raised. Although higher-income tax filers claim a larger average amount of deductions, these tax filers make up a small share of itemizers.

Second, the structure of a limit on itemized deductions could affect which deductions a tax filer might claim. Although a limit based on a percentage reduction in the overall tax benefits of itemized deductions would not change the relative choice of deduction claims, limits based a flat-dollar value cap likely would alter deduction claims and possibly tax filer behavior. This could happen if a tax filer has deductions that exceed a flat-dollar value cap, because the tax filer must make a decision about which deductions to actually claim. Even if a tax filer cannot claim a tax deduction for a particular activity, the tax filer might still engage in the activity for other reasons (although possibly to a lesser extent).

Third, the structure of a limit on itemized deductions also has an effect on its ability to raise revenue. Limiting deductions might raise the taxable income of some individuals, thereby pushing them into a higher marginal tax bracket, and tax a higher share of their income at that higher marginal tax rate. However, certain combinations of deduction limits may shift some tax filers to claim the standard deduction instead of itemizing. In this case, the revenue increase by limiting itemized deduction would be partially offset by more tax filers claiming the standard deduction.

Chapter 3 – Every tax filer has the option to claim deductions when filing their income tax return. Deductions serve four main purposes in the tax code: (1) to account for large, unusual, and necessary personal expenditures, such as extraordinary medical expenses; (2) to encourage certain types of activities, such as homeownership and charitable contributions; (3) to ease the burden of taxes paid to state and local governments; and (4) to adjust for the expenses of earning income, such as unreimbursed employee expenses.

Some tax deductions can be taken by individuals even if they do not itemize. These deductions are commonly referred to as above-the-line deductions, because they reduce a tax filer's adjusted gross income (AGI, or the line). In contrast, itemized and standard deductions are referred to as below-the-line deductions, because they are applied after AGI is calculated to arrive at taxable income.

Tax filers have the option to claim either a standard deduction or to itemize certain deductions. The standard deduction, which is based on filing status, is, among other things, intended to reduce the complexity of paying taxes, as it requires no additional documentation. Alternatively, tax filers claiming itemized deductions must list each item separately on their tax return and be able to provide documentation that the expenditures being deducted have been made. Only tax filers with deductions that can be itemized in excess of the standard deduction find it worthwhile to itemize. Whichever deduction the tax filer claims—standard or itemized—the amount is subtracted from AGI.

Deductions differ from other tax provisions that can reduce a tax filer's final tax liability. Deductions reduce final tax liability by a percentage of the amount deducted, because deductions are calculated before applicable marginal income tax rates. In contrast, tax credits generally reduce an individual's tax liability directly, on a dollar-for-dollar basis, because they are incorporated into tax calculations after marginal tax rates are applied.

Some deductions can only be claimed if they meet or exceed minimum threshold amounts (usually a certain percentage of AGI) in order to simplify tax administration and compliance. In addition, some deductions are subject to a cap (also known as a *ceiling*) in benefits or eligibility. Caps are meant to reduce the extent that tax provisions can distort economic behavior, limit revenue losses, or reduce the availability of the deduction to higher-income tax filers.

Because some tax filers and policymakers may not have detailed knowledge of tax deductions, this report first describes what they are, how they vary in their effects on reducing taxable income, and how they differ from other provisions (e.g., exclusions or credits). Next, a discussion concerning the rationale for deductions as part of the tax code is provided. Because some deductions are classified as tax expenditures, or losses in federal revenue, they might be of interest to Congress from a budgetary perspective. The final section of this report includes tables that summarize each individual tax deduction, under current law. Many of these deductions are part of the permanent income tax code. The American Taxpayer and Relief Act of 2012 (P.L. 112- 240) extended several temporary provisions through 2012 and 2013.

In: Tax Deductions
Editor: Pierre Thibault

ISBN: 978-1-62808-491-7

Chapter 1

RESTRICTIONS ON ITEMIZED TAX DEDUCTIONS: POLICY OPTIONS AND ANALYSIS*

Jane G. Gravelle and Sean Lowry

SUMMARY

The President and leading Members of Congress have indicated that income tax reform is a major policy objective. Some itemized deductions are visible candidates for "broadening the base" of the individual income tax and cutting back on tax expenditures and primarily consist of deductions for mortgage interest, state and local taxes, and charitable contributions. The benefits of itemized deductions are concentrated among higher-income individuals, and that is particularly the case for state and local income tax deductions and charitable deductions.

Proposals for addressing these provisions fall into two general classes. One approach could include repealing or restricting all itemized deductions. A different approach would consider each type of deduction and tailor a reform to the particular objectives and merits of the deductions, such as a lower ceiling on home mortgage interest deduction and a floor for charitable contributions.

This report analyzes various proposals to restrict itemized deductions—both across-the-board and individually tailored—using

---

* This is an edited, reformatted and augmented version of Congressional Research Service, Publication No. R43079, dated May 21, 2013.

standard economic criteria of economic efficiency, distribution, simplicity, and estimated revenue effects. In particular, this report estimates each proposal's potential to contribute to revenue-neutral reductions in income tax rates and the consequences for economic behavior.

Regardless of the class of reform undertaken, for a given revenue target, tax reform involves a trade-off between a broader base and lower income tax rates. One objective of lower rates is presumably to reduce the distortionary effects on labor supply and saving. The analysis in this report, however, shows that this trade off, with respect to effects on labor supply or saving, may be more apparent than real. Economic theory indicates that the tax rate that should determine the supply responses is not the statutory marginal tax rate but the *effective marginal tax rate* (EMTR). If part of the earnings of the last dollar is spent on tax exempt uses, then EMTRs are lower, and eliminating these deductions raises them.

It is possible for a revenue-neutral tax reform to have no effect on EMTRs, or even raise them, which, for some, may defeat the purpose of tax reform. Analysis in this report suggests that eliminating itemized deductions would increase the top EMTR by approximately 41/2 percentage points but permit a statutory rate reduction in a distributionally and revenue-neutral change by about 5 percentage points. Thus, the net effect of this change is a reduction of 1/2 a percentage point (a tenth the size of the statutory reduction). Proposals with ceilings could easily raise EMTRs.

A traditional concern of tax expenditures is generally that they distort economic behavior. However, for each type of deduction there are also some justifications, although the magnitude may be in question. The provision that may have the most support from an economic efficiency standpoint is the deduction for charitable contributions.

Some types of tax reform may simplify the tax code, but others can make it more complex. In addition, transitional rules may be needed for the mortgage interest deduction to limit the impact on taxpayers with large mortgages and to soften the potential impact on the housing market.

INTRODUCTION

The President and some leading Members of Congress have indicated that income tax reform is a major policy objective. The House Budget Resolution (H.Con.Res. 25) supports a revenue-neutral reform that would broaden the individual income tax base and lower statutory income tax rates, while the Senate Budget Resolution (S.Con.Res. 8) proposes revenue raising through base-broadening. The President has proposed substantive tax policy changes in his budget outlines.[1] Further, both tax-writing committees have held hearings and have working groups on tax reform.[2]

Most tax provisions that might be considered for base-broadening are contained in a list of tax expenditures.[3] Itemized deductions are a group of tax expenditures likely to be considered as important candidates for reform. The major itemized deductions are for mortgage interest, state and local taxes, charitable contributions, and medical costs. The Ways and Means Committee has recently held hearings on provisions affecting state and local governments, charitable contributions, and housing tax provisions (including the home mortgage interest deduction).[4]

Itemized deductions account for about one-fifth of all tax expenditures, and may be easy targets of reform, based on their visibility and some policy grounds. In particular, itemized deductions are already listed on the 1040 income tax form and are easily measured. Eliminating some of them might contribute to tax simplification (unlike revisions such as including employee fringe benefits in income). At the same time, itemized deductions have broad support, and are claimed by roughly one-third of tax filers. Arguments can be made to justify some of these deductions and some of them are among the longest-standing provisions of the federal income tax code (see Appendix A for a brief history of itemized deductions).

Reducing incentives and subsidies that alter taxpayers' choices is one potential objective of tax reform. In addition, as suggested by the differing budget resolutions, some proponents of reform see broadening the tax base as a means of raising revenue without raising tax rates, while others see it as a way to pay for reduced tax rates. For a given revenue target, tax reform can involve a trade-off between a broader base and lower rates. In addition, as outlined in this report, base-broadening could have unintended side effects, such as effects on savings incentives or the labor supply.

A variety of proposals for limiting itemized deductions, either as an overall proposition or through specific revisions to certain deductions, have been advanced by policymakers, economists, and tax experts. This report discusses the proposals that have been advanced, their potential revenue gain, their consequences for taxpayer behavior and economic efficiency, their distributional implications, and administrative and transition issues that may arise.

Although this report provides some background material, it assumes some familiarity with itemized tax deductions, and the debate surrounding their reform. For an introduction to tax deductions, see *Tax Deductions for*

Individuals: A Summary, by Sean Lowry. For general tax data analysis on itemized tax deductions, see *Itemized Tax Deductions for Individuals: Data Analysis*, by Sean Lowry.[5]

AN OVERVIEW OF ITEMIZED DEDUCTIONS

Individual income tax filers have the option to claim either a standard deduction or the sum of their itemized deductions on the federal income tax Form 1040. The *standard deduction* is a fixed amount, based on filing status, available to all taxpayers.

Alternatively, tax filers may claim *itemized deductions*. Taxpayers that itemize must list each item separately on their tax return. Whichever deduction a tax filer claims—standard or itemized—the deduction amount is subtracted from adjusted gross income (AGI) in the process of determining taxable income.[6] AGI is the basic measure of income under the federal income tax and is the income measurement before itemized or standard deductions and personal exemptions are taken into account.

Generally, only individuals with aggregate itemized deductions greater than the standard deduction find it worthwhile to itemize.[7] The tax benefit of choosing to itemize is the amount that their itemized deductions exceed the standard deduction, multiplied by their top marginal income tax rate.

About one-third of taxpayers, largely in the middle and upper income parts of the income distribution, itemize deductions. At incomes of more than $200,000, 95% or more of taxpayers itemized, although two-thirds of itemizers had incomes below $100,000. Therefore while the benefits of itemizing are more concentrated in higher incomes, many middle-class taxpayers itemize deductions.[8]

Types of Itemized Deductions

Itemized deductions are often grouped together in broader discussions of tax policy, in part because they are grouped together on the tax Form 1040. But, itemized deductions exist for a variety of reasons, can affect different types of economic behavior, and are designed in ways such that they target (or exclude) different types of tax filers.

One way to distinguish between different types of itemized deductions is whether they are classified as tax expenditures. Tax expenditures are defined under the Congressional Budget and Impoundment Control Act of 1974 (P.L. 93-344) as "revenue losses attributable to provisions of the Federal tax laws which allow a special exclusion, exemption, or deduction from gross income or which provide a special credit, a preferential rate of tax, or a deferral of tax liability."[9] The Joint Committee on Taxation (JCT) also provides annual revenue loss estimates for tax expenditures.[10]

In contrast, some itemized deductions are not classified as tax expenditures because they generally are appropriate to use to measure income (such as employee job expenses).[11] These provisions might be contained in the form of an itemized deduction for reasons of simplifying tax compliance and administration, so that taxpayers do not keep track of and deduct small amounts, or so most taxpayers will not have to encounter provisions that apply to limited numbers of taxpayers on other, simpler, tax forms.

Detailed tables showing the number of claimants and the size of deductions for each type of itemized deduction are shown in the Appendix A. Four basic itemized deductions, summing to $1.1 trillion of deductions in 2010, constitute those classified as tax expenditures:

- State and local deductions for income, sales, and property taxes totaled $442 billion in 2010. Tax deductions for state income taxes were the largest at $246 billion, followed by real estate property taxes at $172 billion. Optional sales tax deductions (which are part of the temporary provisions termed "extenders" and, absent legislation, will expire after 2013) were $16 billion. Tax deductions for state and local personal property taxes (on motor vehicles) were $7 billion.
- Mortgage interest deductions totaled $401 billion in 2010. Less than $2 billion of that amount was for home equity loan points, and less than $7 billion for qualified mortgage insurance premiums. The latter is also an "extender."
- Charitable contribution deductions totaled $172 billion in 2010. Of these deductible contributions, $135 billion was in cash, $44 billion in property, and $31 billion carried over from prior years (due to limits on deductions as a percentage of income).
- Medical and dental expense deductions above the 7.5% floor totaled $85 billion in 2010.

These deductions have diverse purposes. Notably, for example, the deduction of extraordinary medical expenses is not an incentive to encourage spending but a provision to reflect ability to pay taxes. State and local income taxes are not under the control of the taxpayer in the short run (and cannot be avoided other than relocating), but the deduction may encourage state and local governments to enact these taxes. Benefits for homeownership and charitable contributions, however, arise from explicit choices of the taxpayer and are incentives to make the choice to own a home or donate to charity.

Itemized deductions not classified as tax expenditures were $264 billion, although only $117 billion were allowed because many of these deductions are subject, as a group, to a floor and only amounts in excess of 2% of income are deducted. Examples of these itemized deductions (some limited and some not) are investment interest expenses, casualty and theft losses, employee expenses, tax preparation expenses, other costs of earning income, such as investment expenses, and gambling losses. These deductions would likely need to be deducted elsewhere on the tax Form 1040 if itemized deductions were repealed.

Limits on Itemized Deductions and "Pease"

Numerous restrictions are on itemized deductions in the form of floors or ceilings, which may be in dollar amounts or percentage-of-income amounts. A floor means that only deductions in excess of a certain amount are allowed. A ceiling means that only deductions up to a certain amount are allowed. There is also a so called "limitation" on the amount of itemized deductions that certain higher-income tax filers are subject to.[12] Pease applies to tax filers with an AGI over $250,000 ($275,000 for head of household filers and $300,000 for married joint filers). Pease is, however, not a true limit on deductions, but rather an increased tax rate.

Floors and Ceilings

Two itemized deductions are subject to caps or ceilings. Mortgage interest deductions are allowed for interest on the first $1 million of a mortgage. In addition, while interest on home equity loans can be deducted, only interest associated with up to $100,000 of loans is deductible.

Whereas the mortgage interest deduction is subject to a dollar ceiling, charitable contributions are subject to percentage-of-income ceilings, although those ceilings are so high that few taxpayers encounter them. Cash contributions are limited to 50% of income and to 30% of income for contributions to certain types of nonprofits, mainly foundations. These limits are lower for charitable contributions of appreciated property: 30% and 20%.

In effect, the limits prevent individuals from wiping out too much of their tax liability via charitable deductions. Any unused deductions can be also be carried over and deducted in future years.

There is a special provision related to charitable contributions, although not explicitly an itemized deduction, which allows individuals aged 701/2 or older to contribute IRA withdrawals directly to charity without including them in income and then deducting them (if the individual itemizes); this amount is capped at $100,000.

One itemized deduction considered a tax expenditure is subject to a floor: extraordinary medical and dental expenses. Currently, only deductions in excess of 10% of AGI are allowable (7.5% until 2016 for returns where at least one taxpayer is aged 65 or older).[13] Of the itemized deductions not classified as tax expenditures, casualty and theft losses are limited to the excess over $100 and that excess can only be deducted if over 10% of income. Employee expenses, tax preparation expenses and certain other miscellaneous deductions are limited, as a group, to amounts in excess of 2% of income.

The Pease "Limitation"

Some might ask why policymakers would consider new policies to limit itemized deductions when one "already exists" in the form of Pease. Pease, however, is designed in such a way that it is unlikely to have an effect on the value of itemized deductions.

Pease is not a true limit on itemized deductions because it is triggered by an AGI threshold—*not* the amount of deductions claimed. For affected tax filers, the total of certain itemized deductions is reduced by 3% of the amount of AGI exceeding the threshold.[14] The total reduction, however, cannot be greater than 80% of the value of the deductions (and the tax filer always has the option of taking the standard deduction).

Pease's limitations are triggered by an AGI threshold and are implemented like an additional tax rate rather than a true limit on deductions. For a tax filer affected by Pease, a $1.00 increase in AGI will increase taxable income by $1.03 because itemized deductions have been decreased by $0.03 (an increase of itemized deductions of $1 will decrease taxable income by $1). Consequently, the effective marginal tax rate will be 3% higher than the statutory marginal tax rate. For example, a tax filer in the 33% tax bracket faces an effective marginal tax rate of 33.99%—an increase of about 1 percentage point. These effects are not directly linked to deduction claims.

Pease's total reduction (or increase in taxable income) cannot be greater than 80% of the deductions. If this limit were reached then the value of itemized deductions would be affected. Higher-income itemizers are unlikely to hit this 80% limit because some common deductions increase at a rate greater than Pease's 3% surtax. For example, if a tax filer claimed an itemized deduction for state income taxes set at a 5% rate, then the amount claimed for the deduction would increase at a faster rate than the amount of increased taxable income under Pease.

An Overview of Issues and Options for Revision

A range of options could reform or restrict itemized deductions. The options for revisions generally fall into two basic types: overall limits on the size or value of itemized deductions in general through caps, floors, or limits on tax benefit and specific revisions to particular itemized deductions.

These restrictions could be justified in several different ways, including

- to increase federal revenue;
- to allow a reduction in statutory tax rates, while holding revenue constant;
- to reduce economic distortions, where individuals pursue economic behaviors that they would not otherwise do, absent the influences of tax policy (also referred to as *inefficiencies*);
- to increase the progressivity of the federal income tax (an issue of *vertical equity*);
- to reduce discrepancies in the taxation of individuals with similar abilities to pay taxes (also referred to as *horizontal equity*); or
- to simplify the tax code.

This section provides a brief overview of these issues. The subsequent analysis explains the various options and provides more detailed analysis of them considering the issues of revenue, efficiency, distribution, and simplicity.

Revenue Effects

With regard to raising revenue, some might argue that there is less potential revenue to be raised by restricting itemized deductions than from restricting larger tax expenditures.[15] The tax exclusion of employer contributions for health care, exclusion of contributions and earnings to retirement plans, and the reduced tax rates on dividends and long-term capital gains are larger sources of annual revenue loss than the largest itemized deduction (the deduction for home mortgage interest).[16] These options may be limited for a variety of reasons, including difficulties in imputing income (as in the case of the present value of defined-benefit pension plans), difficulties in limiting the effects on middle-class taxpayers (as in the case of employer-provided health benefits), desires to protect savings incentives, or aversions to potential behavioral effects that reduce revenue (as in the case of capital gains).[17]

The maximum revenue gain from an elimination of itemized deductions is projected at $190 billion in 2015, which is 12% of individual income taxes and 44% of the projected deficit under the Congressional Budget Office's (CBO's) standard baseline.[18] Proposals to limit itemized deductions would raise less revenue, in some cases only a small share of the revenue from full elimination.

Effects of Base-Broadening on Marginal Tax Rates, Labor Supply, and Saving

The increasing attention to across-the-board proposals for itemized deductions and, in some cases, other tax expenditures, suggests that the primary focus of base-broadening for some could be the goal of lowering tax rates (or preventing them from rising due to revenue needs) rather than reducing subsidies for undesirable or inefficient activities. Some are interested in keeping statutory tax rates low because they presume that lower rates limit the distorting effects of taxes on wage and capital income, thereby also limiting the effect of taxes on labor supply and savings rates (which are components of long-term growth).

This objective may not be obtainable, as there are many circumstances where restrictions on itemized deductions have similar effects to increases in tax rates; thus base broadening to permit lower rates should not be expected have a supply-side effect. As explained below, it is not the effect of pushing taxpayers into a higher rate bracket, but affecting the tax collected from a marginal dollar of income, which affects taxpayers in the top bracket as well as those in other brackets. This effect is often on the periphery of tax reform discussions, but it is an important issue because designing an efficient proposal to reform itemized deductions that does not lead to significant increases in effective marginal rates may conflict with distributional objectives.

A recent article by Martin Sullivan, Chief Economist at Tax Analysts, argued the narrower point that base-broadening can increase marginal tax rates because, in some cases, because base-broadening expands taxable income enough for some itemizers to push them into higher tax brackets.[19] Of course, this effect would not apply to the highest tax bracket because these tax filers are already being taxed at the top marginal tax rate.

While this effect could certainly be a concern for some, there is a much more important and direct relationship between base-broadening, through restricting itemized deductions, and effective marginal tax rates. Whereas the statutory income tax rates are set in law, the effective tax rates at the margin are the share of an additional dollar of income that is paid in taxes. If part of an additional dollar of earnings is spent in a way that generates a tax deduction, it reduces the *effective marginal tax rate* (EMTR) for that tax filer. If that deduction is eliminated, then the EMTR rises. It is the EMTR—not the statutory tax rate—that could discourage the supply of labor or savings. Despite this potential concern, from a theoretical perspective, prior studies indicate that there is not a consensus among economists whether these marginal effects are statistically or economically significant.[20]

The most straightforward example of this effect is the itemized deduction for state and local income taxes. According to IRS statistics in 2010, the average deduction on itemized returns for state and local income taxes was 5.5% of income for those with an AGI of $200,000 or greater.[21] Because most state income tax rates are progressive, income taxes paid as a share of income would be even higher at the margin. Using an example of 6%, if the federal statutory income tax rate is 35%, and the state income tax is deductible, the total EMTR is 35% plus 6% minus the value of the tax deduction (0.35 times 6%), or 38.9%. If the state and local income tax deduction is eliminated or capped, the EMTR rises to 41% (35% plus 6%). On average then, disallowing the state income tax deduction is the equivalent of raising the EMTR by 2.1 percentage points for those tax filers that would otherwise claim the deduction. Put another way, retaining the state and local deduction and simply raising the federal statutory rate to 37.2% for this bracket would achieve the same effect.[22]

As will be discussed in more detail when specific options are considered, how much of an increase in EMTR occurs depends on the nature of the proposed change, as some approaches are more likely to affect these marginal rates than others, across the various income groups. Similarly some itemized deductions are more likely to have a larger effect on marginal tax rates relative to revenue gain than others.

general idea of what types of taxpayers might be affected. For example, a $17,000 cap would affect most itemizers (approximately 71%), while a $50,000 cap would largely affect itemizers with incomes above $250,000 (totaling approximately 6% of all itemizers).

Table 1. Share of Tax Filers Claiming Itemized Tax Deductions and Average Deduction Claimed, by Adjusted Gross Income (AGI), 2010

Adjusted Gross Income (AGI)	Number of Itemizers	Share of Tax Filers that Itemized	Average Sum of Itemized Deductions Claimed Per Itemizer
$0 under $20k	3,057,363	6%	$15,432
$20k under $50k	10,334,994	23%	$15,810
$50k under $100k	17,258,142	57%	$19,540
$100k under $200k	11,873,957	85%	$27,729
$200k under $250k	1,450,337	95%	$41,079
$250k under $500k	1,866,973	96%	$55,991
$500k under $1million	527,916	97%	$101,502
+$1million	274,826	98%	$443,680

Source: CRS analysis of the Internal Revenue Service's Statistics of Income 2010 in CRS Report R43012, *Itemized Tax Deductions for Individuals: Data Analysis*, by Sean Lowry.

Taxpayers with deductions above the cap would lose the marginal incentives associated with these deductions and their behavior might be affected. After enactment of a flat-cap, deductible activities that are more easily adjustable in the short run (e.g., charitable contributions) could be reduced, which could push other deductions under the limit. Prospective homebuyers might reduce the size of their home purchase or opt for rental housing. Taxpayers with sufficient assets might pay down some or all of their mortgages. Other adjustments, such as mortgages for middle income homeowners or state and local income taxes, may be more difficult to make or make quickly.

Percentage of AGI Caps

Another option to cap itemized deduction amounts would be to restrict total claim amounts to a certain percentage of the tax filer's AGI (hereafter referred to as an "AGI cap"). This option would add complexity to the tax-filing process by requiring an itemizer to additionally calculate their total itemized deduction claims as a share of their AGI.

Compared with the flat dollar-value cap, an AGI cap would be less likely to cause the relative tradeoff effects between claiming certain deductions. Some itemized deductions tend to grow proportionately with income under an AGI cap (such as state and local income taxes) or at slower rate than income.[25]

Table 2 shows the amounts claimed for certain itemized deductions as a share of the total income of itemizers. The total itemized deductions claimed as a share of the total income claimed were less for the higher-income tax filers than those tax filers in the lower or middle sections of the income distribution. Thus, a broad cap on itemized deductions based on AGI cannot be targeted in a way that primarily affects higher-income earners without affecting lower- or middle-income earners.

Table 2. Amount of Itemized Deductions Claimed as a Share of the Income of Itemizers, by Adjusted Gross Income (AGI), 2010

Adjusted Gross Income (AGI)	Home Mortgage Interest	State & Local Sales or Income Taxes	Charitable Gifts	Real Estate Taxes	All Itemized Deductions
$0 under $20k	37.6%	4.3%	8.8%	18.4%	127.8%
$20k under $50k	15.5%	1.1%	4.5%	6.1%	43.6%
$50k under $100k	10.3%	0.9%	3.1%	4.0%	26.6%
$100k under $200k	7.8%	1.0%	2.6%	3.3%	20.5%
$200k under $250k	6.3%	1.6%	2.5%	3.0%	18.5%
$250k under $500k	4.9%	2.2%	2.4%	2.6%	16.8%
$500k under $1million	2.9%	2.9%	2.6%	1.9%	15.0%
+$1million	0.6%	6.1%	4.0%	0.8%	13.4%
All Itemizers	7.2%	4.8%	3.1%	3.1%	22.1%

Source: CRS analysis of the Internal Revenue Service's Statistics of Income 2010, Table 2.1- Returns with Itemized Deductions: Sources of Income, at http://www.irs.gov/uac/SOI—-Individual-Statistical-Tablesby-Size-of-Adjusted-Gross-Income.

The data in **Table 2** show that some itemized deductions comprise a larger share of income of higher-income earners. If a policy goal is to minimize the negative effects of a cap on middle-income tax filers, an AGI cap could be applied only to certain deductions, such as the deduction for state and local taxes or charitable gifts in order to reduce the effect of the cap on itemizers in the middle of the income distribution.

Tax Benefit Value Caps

Another way to restrict itemized deductions is by limiting the value of certain provisions rather than the claims. In contrast to limits on deduction *claims* (which would be calculated *before* applying the progressive statutory income tax rates), a limit on the *value* (tax benefit to the tax filer) of certain tax provisions would be calculated *after* applying their tax rates. That is, one approach limits the deductions taken, while the other limits the effect of those deductions on tax liability. Two types of restrictions have been suggested: limiting the marginal tax rate at which deductions are valued or limiting the total value of itemized deductions to a percentage of income.

Restrictions on the tax value of deductions tend to affect tax filers facing higher marginal income tax rates (than those facing lower marginal tax rates) because the tax value of itemized deductions increases as marginal rates increase.[26]

Limiting the Tax Rate at Which Deductions are Valued

In his FY2014 budget recommendation, President Obama proposed limiting the tax rate that applies to itemized deductions, certain above-the-line deductions, and certain income exclusions to 28% for tax filers in the top three brackets (33%, 35%, and 39.6%).[27] Taxpayers affected would generally be those with incomes of $250,000 or more. Earlier budget outlines had proposed these restrictions for itemized deductions only.[28]

Limiting the Total Value of Deductions as a Share of Income

Researchers Martin Feldstein, Dan Feenberg, and Maya Maguineas (2011) proposed another option (hereafter referred to as “FFM”) to limit the total value that certain tax expenditures, including itemized deductions, can reduce one’s tax burden as a share of AGI.[29] The initial FFM proposal called for limiting the value of certain tax expenditures to 2% of a tax filer’s AGI. Specifically, FFM would apply only to the sum of (1) total itemized deductions, (2) the exclusion for health insurance costs, and (3) a number of tax credits (e.g., the child tax credit). The researchers chose these tax provisions because they are among some of the largest tax expenditures in the federal income tax code. According to Martin Feldstein, the goal of this proposal is to both enhance progressivity in the tax system and reduce tax expenditures (i.e., the loss of revenue), among other things, without changes to the statutory tax rates.[30]

If applied to the itemized deductions alone, this provision would limit deductions more for higher-income taxpayers than the limit on deductions as a percentage of income. Limiting the value of itemized deductions to 2% of income would be the equivalent of limiting deductions for taxpayers in the 15% bracket to 13.3% (because 0.15 times 13.3% equals 2%), whereas for taxpayers in the top bracket, it would be equivalent to a 5% limit (2% dividend by 0.396).

The original FFM proposal has since been amended by the Committee for a Responsible Federal Budget (CRFB) to include additional policy options to focus on higher-income tax filers.[31] The rationale for this targeted approach is that more than 40% of tax expenditures accrue to those with annual incomes above $200,000.[32] These options include a $10,000 flat-cap; phasing in FFM for tax filers earning between $250,000 and $500,000; or including additional tax expenditures under the original FFM proposal.[33]

Floors

As noted earlier some itemized deductions can only be claimed if they meet or exceed minimum threshold amounts (usually a certain percentage of AGI) in order to simplify tax administration and compliance or confine deductions to extraordinary expenditures. An option that could raise revenue while preserving the marginal incentives in many cases is an overall floor, with deductions allowed only in excess of that amount. The floor could be a dollar floor or a percentage of income floors. As implied by data in Table 1 and Table 2 dollar floors are more restrictive for lower-income itemizers, whereas percentage of income floors would proportionally reduce deductions more at the higher-income levels. For example, a 5% floor would eliminate, for the average taxpayer in the $1 million or more income class, 37% of deductions, whereas it would eliminate 24% of deductions in the $100,000 to $200,000 class.

Although a floor is an across-the-board option, it has more frequently been proposed for specific provisions whose marginal effects are more likely to be considered desirable, such as charitable contributions.

Convert Deductions to Credits

One option for reforming itemized deductions is to convert them into credits. Proponents of converting deductions to credits argue that credits are fairer than deductions because a taxpayer that faces a lower marginal tax rate benefits less from a deduction than a taxpayer facing a higher marginal tax rate, even if they have identical expenses (e.g., the same mortgage interest expenses).[34] On the other hand, opponents of converting deductions to credits argue that the reduced value of the tax preference (particularly for higher-income individuals) might reduce the incentives for certain individuals to engage in, what some believe, are desirable activities. Credits could be structured as non-refundable or refundable.[35] In the case of a refundable credit, the dollar-for-dollar reduction in tax liability is the same regardless of a taxpayer's marginal tax rate—even if the taxpayer has no tax liability.

If credits are allowed for all taxpayers, those taking the standard deduction would also qualify and this extension of benefits would limit any revenue gains as well as complicate tax filing. Credits could be restricted to those who do not take the standard deduction, however.

Some argue that the choice between structuring tax provisions as deductions or credits should depend on the purpose of the deduction. If the purpose is to correct for ability to pay taxes, then a deduction may be appropriate.[36] If the purpose is to encourage certain types of behavior (e.g., charitable contributions), it is less clear whether credits or deductions would be the preferred method. If tax filers have a greater response to tax subsidies at higher incomes, it could be more efficient to use deductions to present lower after-tax prices for these taxpayers.

Elimination or Proportional Cutbacks of All Itemized Deductions

Eliminating all itemized deductions could reduce tax compliance costs for tax filers, potentially reduce some economic inefficiencies, and eliminate the unequal value of itemized deductions between tax filers facing higher marginal tax rates compared with tax filers facing lower tax rates.

Although cases can be made for restricting, reforming, or even eliminating certain itemized deductions, the variety of justifications for itemized deductions makes it difficult to make a compelling argument for eliminating *all* itemized deductions.

The 2010 *Chairmen's Mark* of the President's National Commission on Fiscal Responsibility and Reform (hereafter referred to as "Simpson-Bowles") calls for an elimination of all itemized deductions, and a conversion of selected tax expenditures to credits.[37] Simpson-Bowles would still allow taxpayers to claim a standard deduction and any personal exemptions for dependents.[38] Deductions for mortgage interest and charitable contributions would be replaced with 12% nonrefundable tax credits available for all tax filers.[39] Only charitable contributions in excess of 2% of income would be eligible for the credit.

The Domenici-Rivlin (D-R) Debt Reduction Task Force also calls for an elimination of itemized deductions, while converting selected tax expenditures into refundable tax credits.[40] Specifically, the D-R proposal would allow all taxpayers to claim a 20% credit for home mortgage interest expenses on a principal residence up to $25,000. The mortgage interest credit would then be phased down from 20% to 15% over five years. The D-R proposal would also allow a 15% refundable credit for charitable contributions.

The D-R proposal also calls for changes in tax administration in areas that are currently in the form of an itemized deduction, such that mortgage brokers and charities apply to the IRS for a matching grant to supplement payments from taxpayers. For example, for every $85 a taxpayer gives, the charity would receive another $15 or mortgage lenders will apply for a tax credit, which would be passed through to homeowners as a 15% reduction in their home mortgage interest payments. The purpose of structuring the D-R tax credit in this manner, according to its authors, is to reduce the need for certain individuals to file a tax return, thereby possibly reducing tax administration costs.

Even if policymakers find the original intent of itemized deductions no longer desirable, elimination of all itemized deductions that are not considered tax expenditures would change the base of income that is subject to tax. Individuals with catastrophic medical expenses would find their taxes rising perhaps beyond their ability to pay. Provision might need to be made to deduct these items elsewhere.

Rather than eliminate itemized deductions, a percentage could be disallowed. For example, if 20% of deductions are disallowed, the value of an additional dollar of deductions would be reduced by 20%.

OPTIONS FOR REFORMS OF SPECIFIC PROVISIONS

Rather than an across-the-board limit on itemized deductions, each individual provision could be considered. Specific tax expenditures might be eliminated, or limited. The following subsections discuss some options that have been discussed in past tax reform debates for the three major categories of itemized deductions: mortgage interest, state and local taxes (including real estate property taxes), and charitable contributions. These categories represent three of the four general categories of itemized deductions that are considered tax expenditures. The floor for the fourth category, the deduction for extraordinary medical expenses, was increased recently.[41] Thus, this remaining provision has not generally been the target of additional, specific reforms.

Mortgage-Related Deductions

The itemized deduction for home mortgage interest expenses is currently limited to interest on the first $1 million of mortgage debt, combined on a primary and secondary residence, and first $100,000 of home equity debt.[42]

Three types of specific limits on these components of the home mortgage interest deduction could be considered. First, the current $1 million cap on mortgages eligible for interest deductions could be reduced, with $500,000 the number most commonly cited. A declining limit might also be used to eliminate the provision over time.[43] Secondly, the mortgage interest deduction could be limited to primary residences and not extended to second, or vacation homes, as in current law. Finally, interest on home equity loans could be disallowed; or the ceiling on those whose interest is deductible (currently $100,000) may be reduced. Growth in deductions of home equity loans has been perceived to be related to the Tax Reform Act of 1986 (P.L. 99-514), which ended the deduction for consumer interest other than mortgages. In part due to this tax policy, home equity lines of credit have become a substitute, to some extent, for consumer interest.[44]

The deduction for qualified mortgage insurance premiums, which might be considered in the nature of interest, is part of the "tax extenders," temporary provisions that tend to get extended every year or two. This provision, along with other extender provisions, could be allowed to lapse.

Credits for interest paid on home mortgages would allow all homeowners with mortgages to benefit, even those who do not itemize, but because the credit extends benefits to a wider class of (mostly lower-income) taxpayers, it would likely raise less revenue and add to complexity for those additional taxpayers. It is possible, depending on the rate chosen, that a credit could result in a net revenue loss, if the value of the tax credits from new homeowners exceeds the revenue gain from higher-income tax filers whose deductions were taken at higher rates.

As noted earlier, the D-R proposal includes a matching grant for mortgage lenders to be passed along to individuals, as a substitute for the mortgage deduction.

State and Local Tax Deductions

The federal itemized deduction for state and local taxes includes state and local income, real estate, and personal property taxes. An option to choose a deduction for state and local sales taxes in lieu of the deduction for state and local income taxes is part of the extenders, which is temporarily in effect through 2013.[45]

Each of the state and local tax deductions might be separately considered. For example, sales taxes were eliminated as a deduction in 1986, and have been introduced as an alternative deduction option only recently and also temporarily.[46] That option could be allowed to lapse permanently. Another deduction that might be eliminated is the deduction for personal property taxes, which are generally taxes on motor vehicles. They are not imposed in many states, such as those states where taxes might be collected on motor vehicles based on weight (and thus, not deductible). Deductions for personal property taxes are claimed by a much smaller number of tax filers than the deduction for state and local income taxes (see Table A-1 in the Appendix A).

The deductions for state and local income, sales, and property taxes cover many tax filers and might be considered for more limited reforms. A cap on deductions based on a percent of adjusted gross income ("AGI cap") has been more frequently proposed than a flat-dollar cap because income taxes tend to grow constantly with income, and a dollar cap may be considered to be too harsh (especially if the flat-cap is not indexed for inflation over time). According to Table 2, claims for the deduction for state and local income or sales taxes can be limited by an AGI cap in such a way that it primarily targets certain tax filers. For example, a 3% cap would largely focus the restriction on those with $500,000 or more of income.

Charitable Contributions

For many proposals relating to charitable contributions, a key policy concern for some is to retain the giving incentives. Thus, revision of the deduction for charitable contributions is more likely to involve floors than ceilings. A floor would only allow deductions of contributions in excess of a dollar amount or percentage of income. This approach would raise revenue while preserving more of the marginal incentive to give. It would also eliminate deductions for small amounts and the associated record-keeping.

As with mortgage interest, proposals have been made to convert the charitable contributions deduction into a credit. If allowed for non-itemizers as well, it would increase complexity and limit the revenue-raising capacity of the change. The D-R plan proposed to provide grants to charities as a substitute for credits to simplify tax administration.

Reforms for the deduction for charitable contributions could be directed specifically at gifts of property, both property that has lost value (such as clothes, household items, and automobiles) and property that has appreciated (such as art, stocks, and real estate). Overall, according to IRS statistics, gifts of property account for 26% of contributions in 2010.[47] Gifts of household items and clothes accounted for 7%, or about a quarter of the total gifts of property.[48] Gifts of appreciated property tend to be more concentrated among higher-income tax payers, while gifts of household items and clothes are probably more common among middle-class taxpayers.

For property without an easily established value (such as household items, clothes, art, and perhaps to some degree real estate) there is an incentive for tax filers to overstate the value so that they can claim a larger deduction.[49] For the gifts of clothes and household items, a separate floor, a dollar ceiling, disallowing the deduction, or allowing the deduction of only a fraction of the market value are possible options to restrict the provision. The Joint Committee on Taxation (JCT), for example, proposed a $500 limit on these deductions.[50] Allowing deduction of a fraction of the value might be sufficient to encourage donations rather than discarding these items.

Gifts of appreciated property, which account for three-quarters of the total of gifts of property, present more complex challenges. These donations have two benefits: first, the market value is deductible, and second, the difference between initial cost (basis) and market value if the asset were sold and donated as cash is *not* taxed as a capital gain. For assets not regularly traded (i.e., difficult to price), there is an incentive to exaggerate the value to claim a larger deduction. About 40% of these gifts of appreciated property are in stocks, about 15% are in real estate and property easements, and 3% in arts and collectibles.[51]

More even treatment between cash and property gifts could be obtained by imposing the capital gains tax on the appreciation of charitable gifts. A stricter treatment would disallow deduction except for the basis (generally, cost of the property). Effectively, this would disallow deductions for appreciation in the value. This change would encourage the taxpayer to sell the asset and then donate the cash proceeds, which would increase the value of the charitable deduction to the taxpayer. This treatment would also deal with the problems of over-valuation by providing incentives for the individual to find a market price for the item.

Two tax extender provisions are also associated with charitable contributions that might be considered if the itemized deduction for charitable contributions is revised. One extender allows individuals who are 701/2-years-old to donate distributions from individual retirement accounts (IRAs) directly to charity without including them in their calculations of gross income.[52] This income exclusion treatment benefits non-itemizers, and also reduces AGI and the likelihood of being taxed on Social Security benefits. If this provision were left intact, it might allow some individuals to circumvent floors or ceilings. A second extender deals with treatment of conservation property.[53]

Because charitable contributions are often viewed as desirable, there are many proposals to expand the benefit, such as extending the deduction to non-itemizers (as an above-the-line deduction), allowing deductions for a particular calendar year to be made up until taxes are due on April 15 of the following year, allowing lottery winners to contribute their winnings to charity without being taxed, and expanding the allowances for direct contributions from IRAs.[54]

REVENUE ESTIMATES FOR PROPOSALS TO RESTRICT ITEMIZED DEDUCTIONS

This section of the report presents revenue estimates for proposals to restrict itemized deductions, where available. To provide a better idea of how these changes might contribute to any base-broadening goals for tax reform, revenue gains from each proposal are converted into equivalent across-the board rate reductions that would retain revenue neutrality, as well as the potential percentage point reduction in the highest and lowest rates.

Consider first the effects of eliminating some or all of the itemized deductions. Table 3 shows the Tax Policy Center's (TPC) revenue estimates for eliminating itemized deductions in 2015 based on estimated benefits. For example, eliminating all itemized deductions is estimated to increase revenue by $190.1 billion in 2015. If this revenue increase were used to offset revenue losses associated with a reduction in statutory tax rates, then the elimination of all itemized deductions could lead to a 10.6% across-the-board reduction in statutory tax rates (if distributed evenly across all of the marginal tax brackets). In other words, the top, statutory marginal tax bracket could be lowered by 4.2 percentage points from 39.6% to 35.4% and the lowest, statutory marginal tax bracket could be lowered by 1.1 percentage points from 10% to 8.9%.[55]

Table 3. Revenue Gain and Tax Reduction Estimates for Eliminating of Itemized Deductions, 2015

Provision	Revenue Gains (in Billions)	Reduction in Statutory Tax Rate	Point Reduction in Top Rate (39.6%)	Point Reduction in Bottom Rate (10%)
Mortgage Interest	$79.6	4.7%	1.9	0.5
Mortgage Interest and Real Estate Taxes	$100.5	5.9%	2.3	0.6
All State and Local Taxes	$95.5	5.6%	2.2	0.6
Charitable Gifts	$49.7	3.0%	1.2	0.3
All Itemized Deductions	$190.1	10.6%	4.2	1.1

Sources: CRS analysis of data from the Tax Policy Center (TPC), Congressional Budget Office (CBO), and Joint Committee on Taxation (JCT). Estimates of Revenue come from TPC, Tables T13-0077, 0079, 0095, 0097, 0099, at http://taxpolicycenter.org/numbers/listdocs.cfm?BrowseTPC=true; data on revenues for FY2015 comes from CBO, *The Budget and Economic and Outlook: Fiscal Years 2013-2023*, February 5, 2013, at http://www.cbo.gov/publication/43907; and data on credits in revenues comes from JCT, *Estimate Of Federal Tax Expenditures For Fiscal Years 2012-2017*, JCS-1-13, February 1, 2013, at https://www.jct.gov/publications.html?func=startdown&id=4504.

Notes: Calculations for reductions in tax rate are based on the formula $t_n(1+x) = t$, where t_n is the new tax rate, t is the old tax rate, and x is the revenue gain divided by revenues before credits. Note also that a tax expenditure is not necessarily the same as a revenue loss, due to behavioral effects and potential interactions.

Table 4 shows the JCT estimates for the revenue loss in 2015 for each itemized deduction classified as a tax expenditure, including the deduction for medical expenses. JCT also separates real estate taxes from others itemized deductions, leaving a tax expenditure estimate for the remaining state taxes; as noted below, about 98% of that provision is for income taxes, and the remainder of the tax expenditure estimate is for personal property taxes (sales tax deductions would have expired at that point, under current law).

Table 4. Estimates of Tax Expenditures for Itemized Deductions, 2015

Provision	Revenue Gains (in Billions)	Reduction in Statutory Tax Rate	Point Reduction in Top Rate (39.6%)	Point Reduction in Bottom Rate (10%)
Mortgage Interest	$75.0	4.5%	1.8	0.5
Real Estate Taxes	$30.4	1.9%	0.7	0.2
Other State and Local Taxes	$58.6	3.5%	1.4	0.4
Charitable Gifts	$45.1	2..8%	1.1	0.3
Medical Expenses	$14.2	0.9%	0.4	0.1

Source: CRS analysis of Joint Committee on Taxation, Estimate Of Federal Tax Expenditures For Fiscal Years 2012-2017, JCS-1-13, February 1, 2013, at https://www.jct.gov/publications.html?func=startdown&id=4504.

Notes: Calculations for reductions in tax rate are based on the formula tn(1+x) = t, where tn is the new tax rate, t is the old tax rate, and x is the revenue gain divided by revenues before credits.

Table 5 provides revenue estimates for 2015, largely drawn from the TPC, for a variety of across-the-board limits to itemized deductions, including dollar ceilings, limiting the value to 2% of adjusted gross income (FFM), and limiting the value at which the deductions can be taken to 15% and 28% (i.e., similar to the President's budget proposal for FY2014). Because some view charitable deductions as provisions that should be protected, some options exclude restricting them.

Table 6 provides estimated revenue effects in 2015 for a number of specific options that were discussed earlier for the three major itemized deductions: mortgage interest, charitable contributions, and state and local taxes. As the estimates indicate, some minor proposals would yield modest amounts of revenue. On the other hand, some options could result in significant increases in revenue, such as ceilings on the mortgage interest deduction and the floors on the charitable deduction.

Table 5. Revenue Estimates From Across-the Board Restrictions on Itemized Deductions, 2015

Provision	Revenue Gains (in billions)[a]	Reduction in Statutory Tax Rate[b]	Point Reduction in Top Rate (39.6%)	Point Reduction in Bottom Rate (10%)
Eliminate All Itemized Deductions	$183[c]	4.7	4.1	0.5
Eliminate All Itemized Deductions, Excluding Charity	$104	6.1	2.4	0.6
$17,000 Flat-Cap	$144	5.9	2.3	0.6
$25,000 Flat-Cap	$104	5.6	2.2	0.6
$50,000 Flat-Cap	$59	3.0	1.2	0.3
$17,000 Flat-Cap, Excluding Charity	$70	4.2	1.6	0.4
$25,000 Flat-Cap, Excluding Charity	$59	3.5	1.4	0.4
$50,000 Flat-Cap, Excluding Charity	$38	2.3	0.9	0.2
Limit Value of Benefit to 2% of AGI,	$135	7.8	3.1	0.8
Limit Value of Benefit to 2% of AGI, Excluding Charity	$106	6.2	2.4	0.6
Limit Deduction Value to 15% Rate	$120	7.0	2.8	0.7
Limit Deduction Value to 28% Rate	$27	1.7	0.7	0.2
Limit Deduction Value to 28% Rate, Excluding Charity	$17	1.1	0.4	0.1

Sources: For all provisions except limiting to the 15% rate, Tax Policy Center Estimates of Provisions, 2012 Tables (T12-0300, 0326, 0273, 0362, 0359, 0361), at http://www.taxpolicycenter.org/numbers/index.cfm. For the 15% Rate, Congressional Budget Office, Reducing the Deficit: Spending and Revenue Options, March 2011, at http://www.cbo.gov/sites/default/files/cbofiles/ftpdocs /120xx/doc12085/03-10-reducingthedeficit.pdf.

[a] Some estimates may be lowered or raised because of the revisions in tax rates and slight variations may arise depending on the date of the estimate.

[b] Calculations for reductions in tax rate are based on the formula $tn(1+x) = t$, where tn is the new tax rate, t is the old tax rate, and x is the revenue gain divided by revenues before credits.

[c] This revenue estimate differs from the estimate for "eliminate all itemized deductions" in Table 3 because the estimates were prepared by the Tax Policy Center at different times, using different baselines.

Table 6. Revenue Effects of Modifications of Specific Itemized Deductions, 2015

Itemized Deduction Provision	Revenue Gains (in billions)	Percentage Point Reduction in Statutory Tax Rates	Percentage Point Reduction in Top Rate (39.6% Rate)	Point Reduction in Bottom Rate (10% Rate)
Mortgage Interest				
Replace Deduction with a 15% Credit	$17	1.0	0.4	0.1
Change Limit from $1,000,000 to $500,000	$15	0.9	0.4	0.1
Disallow Deduction for Secondary Residences	$1	0.1	0.0	0.0
Permanently Disallow Insurance Premiums	$1	0.1	0.0	0.0
Charitable Contributions				
2% Of AGI Floor	$21	1.3	0.5	0.1
$500/$1,000 Floor[a]	$6	0.4	0.1	0.0
Replace Deduction with a 15% credit	$14	0.9	0.3	0.1
Limit Property Gifts to Deduction of Basis	$2	0.1	0.0	0.0
Disallow Clothes, Household Items	$2	0.1	0.0	0.0
Permanently Disallow Contributions from IRA[b]	$1	0.1	0.0	0.0
State and Local Taxes				
2% of AGI Ceiling	$66	4.0	1.6	0.4
$5,000 Ceiling (In 2008 Dollars, Indexed)	$58	3.5	1.4	0.4
Replace Deduction with a 15% Credit	$25	1.5	0.6	0.3
Eliminate Personal Property Tax Deduction	$1	0.1	0.0	0.0
Permanently Disallow Sales Tax Option	$3	0.2	0.1	0.0

Sources: Estimates for mortgage interest credit and ceiling estimates from the Tax Policy Center Tables T13- 0100, T13-0103, T11-0013, at http://www.taxpolicycenter.org/numbers/index.cfm; estimates for disallowing deductions for mortgage interest on second homes from Committee for a Responsible Federal Government, *Raising Revenue from Higher Earners through Base Broadening*, November 15, 2012, at http://crfb.org/sites/default/ files/raising_revenue_from_higher_earners_11_15-2.pdf; estimates for mortgage insurance premiums and other extenders (e.g., sales tax and charitable donations from IRAs) from Joint Committee on Taxation (JCT), *Estimated Revenue Effects Of The Revenue*

Provisions Contained In An Amendment In The Nature Of A Substitute To H.R. 8, The "American Taxpayer Relief Act Of 2012," As Passed By The Senate On January 1, 2013, JCX-1-13, at https://www.jct.gov /publications.html?func=startdown&id=4497;

Estimates for charitable contributions 2% floor and state and local tax 2% ceiling and limits to basis on gifts of property provisions from Congressional Budget Office (CBO), *Reducing the Deficit: Spending and Revenue Options*, March 2011, at http://www.cbo.gov/sites/default/files/cbofiles/ftpdocs/120xx/doc12085/03-10-reducingthedeficit.pdf; CBO, *Budget Options*, Volume 2, August 2009, at http://www.cbo.gov/publication/41190. For the dollar floor and 15% credit for charitable contributions, see CBO, *Options for Changing the Tax Treatment of Charitable Giving*, May 2011, at http://www.cbo.gov/sites/default /files/cbofiles/ ftpdocs/121xx/doc12167/ charitablecontributions.pdf; and Estimates for disallowing deductions of clothes and household items were based on Testimony of C. Eugene Steuerle before the Ways and Means Committee, on Tax Reform and Charitable Contributions, February 13, 2013, at http:// waysandmeans. house.gov/uploadedfiles/steuerletestimony02.14.2013fc.pdf.

Estimates for converting state and local deductions to credits and for dollar caps are based on CBO, *The Deductibility of State and Local Taxes*, February 2008, at http://www.cbo.gov/publication/41647. Estimates for eliminating personal property tax are from Testimony of C. Eugene Steuerle before the Ways and Means Committee, on Tax Reform and Charitable Contributions, February 13, 2013, at http://waysandmeans.house.gov/ uploadedfiles/steuerletestimony02.14. 2013fc.pdf., based on share of tax expenditure for state income and personal property totals in Appendix A.

[a] The dollar floor and 15% credit were estimated for 2006 and were increased by 10% to be compatible with current charitable contribution estimates.

[b] Note that the revenue estimate for contribution for capital gains real property for conservation purposes, the other extender, was too small (<$0.1 billion) to include in the table.

EFFECTS OF BASE-BROADENING ON EFFECTIVE MARGINAL TAX RATES

As noted earlier, the increasing attention towards analysis of across-the-board proposals for itemized deductions and, in some cases, other tax expenditures, suggests that the primary focus of base-broadening for some could be the goal of lowering tax rates (or preventing them from rising due to revenue needs) rather than reducing subsidies for undesirable or inefficient activities. However, restricting tax provisions causes effective marginal rates to rise and could defeat the purpose of base-broadening to lower tax rates. This section discusses this issue for several types of revisions.

The effective marginal rate is affected by tax-free uses of income, many of which are embodied in itemized deductions and affect the marginal rate on all types of income (e.g., wage, investment, self-employment). In the illustrations in this section, the calculations do not take into account the reductions in effective marginal rates for all tax expenditures that might have marginal effects or the lower tax rates on capital gains. Therefore, they should be seen as an illustration of what would occur for a taxpayer whose only tax benefits are itemized deductions.

Not all itemized deductions have a marginal effect at every point along the income distribution. Some insight can be gained by looking at the pattern of deductions across income classes. If a deduction rises as income rises, it is likely that the deduction is not only marginal (affecting the last dollar of income) across all incomes, but is also higher at the margin than on average. As shown in, Table 7 and in the earlier Table 2, of the four major itemized deductions, the share of returns and AGI for two deductions tends to rise with income at almost every class over an AGI of $200,000: state income taxes and charitable gifts. If deductions rise as a share of income, the implication is that the deduction out of each marginal dollar is growing, and thus the elimination of deductions would increase effective taxation at the margin even in a revenue neutral tradeoff for lower statutory rates. If this share is falling, the deduction at the margin is smaller than the average deduction and could be zero. The mortgage interest deduction tends to decline with income at very high income levels (e.g., $10 million), which is not surprising as higher-income tax filers generally do not need to borrow as much (as a share of their income) to purchase their homes. In addition, homes may be a smaller part of these tax filers' budgets, which is also reflected in the declining value of property tax deduction claims as a share of AGI. In general, itemized deductions are a smaller percentage of itemizers' AGI as income rises.

Outside of itemized deductions other provisions may involve tax-exempt income because of exclusions from income. For example, employer-provided benefits such as health insurance and pensions (or similar benefits for the self-employed) reduce the effective marginal tax rate on earnings from wages or self-employment. However, some of these benefits, for example, tax exclusions for health insurance, are unlikely to increase with income on average, especially when income grows to very high levels. Pension benefits are more likely to be marginal because pensions are related to income. Other benefits, such as tax-exempt state and local bonds are more likely to rise with income and be marginal in some cases because these bonds are more attractive to taxpayers with higher tax rates.

Table 7. Itemized Deductions for Returns that Itemize, 2010

	Share of Deductions	Share of Adjusted Gross Income (AGI)		
Itemized Deduction	**Returns with an AGI Less Than $200k**	**All Returns**	**Returns with an AGI Greater Than $200k**	**Returns with an AGI Greater Than $10m**
State and Local Income	48%	4.8%	5.5%	5.2%
Real Estate Tax	72%	3.1%	1.8%	0.2%
Mortgage Interest	83%	7.2%	3.0%	0.1%
Charitable Gifts	59%	3.1%	2.9%	5.5%
All Itemized Deductions	72%	22.1%	15.3%	13.2%

Source: CRS calculations based on data obtained from Internal Revenue Service, Statistics of Income, Individual Income Tax Returns with Itemized Deductions, at http://www.irs.gov/uac/SOI—Individual-StatisticalTables-by-Size-of-Adjusted-Gross-Income.

Table 7 also shows another potential issue with base-broadening through restricting itemized deductions: the "costs" of base-broadening might be concentrated among middle-income itemizers whereas the tax benefits of statutory rate reductions could spread across *all* tax filers.[56] In all cases, a large share of these itemized deductions is on tax returns that have an AGI less than $200,000. Thus, if the policy goal is to protect middle-income itemizers from increased tax burdens through high ceilings, potential revenue gains are limited. For high-income taxpayers, who retain an average, but not a marginal, benefit from itemized deductions, the statutory rate reductions to keep their burden fixed would be too small to offset the rise in effective marginal tax rates from the loss of deductions at the margin. If ceilings are lowered to increase revenue and permit higher top statutory rate reductions, the burden on middle class taxpayers would increase. To avoid that effect, intermediate rates would have to be reduced, leaving less revenue for reducing the top rate (or rates).

Effects of Across-the-Board Options to Restrict Itemized Deductions on Effective Marginal Tax Rates

As is the case with restricting individual itemized deductions provisions, some of the across-the-board options for base-broadening through restrictions on itemized deductions have consequences for effective marginal tax rates (EMTRs). As previously mentioned, the EMTR is affected by tax-free uses of income, many of which are embodied in itemized deductions and which affect the marginal rate on all types of income. The calculations in the analysis and examples in the following section of this report do not take into account the reductions in EMTRs for all tax expenditures that might have marginal effects or the lower tax rates on capital gains. Nor do these calculations account for Medicare taxes, including those taxes on capital income enacted by the Patient Protection and Affordable Care Act (PPACA; P.L. 111-148, as amended).[57] Therefore, this analysis is only an illustration of what could occur for a taxpayer whose only benefits are itemized deductions and whose only tax is the income tax.

Table 8. Illustration of Top Effective Marginal Tax Rate Increases (assuming 5.5% in state income tax deductions and 5.5% in charitable deductions)

Revision	Percentage Point Increase in Effective Marginal Tax Rate
Eliminate All Deductions	4.4
Cap at $17,000	4.4
Cap at $50,000	4.4
Cap at 6% of AGI	2.0
2% Limit on Value	2.4
Allow at 28% Rate/28% Credit Instead of Deduction	1.3
15% Credit Instead of Deduction	2.7
Eliminate State and Local Income Tax	2.2
Eliminate Charitable Deductions	2.2
Eliminate Mortgage Interest Deduction	0.0
Eliminate Real Estate Tax Deduction	0.0

Source: CRS calculations, see text for discussion of calculations.

Table 8 provides illustrative effects of certain proposals to restrict itemized tax deductions on EMTRs for the top rate and a very high income taxpayer. These effects do not refer to any particular income level, but one high enough that the tax rate is at 39.6% (which applies to taxable income of joint returns with $450,000 or more income) and one where the assumptions regarding charitable contributions and taxes are appropriate (well in excess of $1million).[58]

Eliminating Some or All Itemized Deductions

Eliminating itemized deductions could raise EMTRs for tax filers across a broad range of income. As the discussion above suggests, elimination of entire categories of deductions could be problematic for some because tax filers of a wide-range of income tend to claim certain itemized deductions. Even those deductions where returns with an AGI less than $200,000 have lower claim amounts as a share of income (state and local income or sales taxes, followed by charitable contributions) have more than half of the benefit fall in lower incomes. These deductions are still likely to be marginal and increase marginal tax rates for lower-income tax filers.

For example, for a tax filer in the 25% bracket who might have marginal deductions of those in the $100,000 to $200,000 class (based on **Table 2** where deductions are 20.5% of income would have an increase in effect rate of 5.1 percentage points (0.205 times 0.25). Eliminating taxes, mortgage interest, and charity, which account for almost 15% of income would increase rates by 3.7 percentage points with most of the increase due to provisions associated with housing (mortgage interest and real property taxes). For taxpayers in the top bracket and at very high income levels (as shown in **Table 8**), the deductions that are marginal are probably around 11%, half from taxes and half from charity, leading to a 4.4 percentage point increase.

Flat Dollar Cap on Itemized Deductions

A flat-cap approach could direct more of the revenue increase to higher-income tax filers (although heterogeneity across returns means it would not be possible to confine the effects solely to higher incomes). If the policy goal is to concentrate the effects in the highest income classes, then the dollar cap would have to be set high. According to the data in Table 1, a flat-cap would have to be around $50,000 to largely confine the effects to taxpayers with $250,000 or more in income (most itemized returns with high incomes are joint returns). According to Table 8, returns in the $100,000 to $200,000 income range have average deductions of 20.5% of AGI and returns in the $200,000 to $250,000 AGI range have 18.5%, so that a dollar cap equal to around 20% of the $250,000 AGI level would be needed.

Still, a flat-cap could lead to the marginal effects discussed, above. Taxpayers with incomes over $200,000 would have reduced deductions of around 8% at a minimum (based on shares for charity and state income taxes in Table 7). These reduced deductions would raise effective marginal tax rates on average by about 3 percentage points. For very high income tax filers, it would eliminate on average about 11% of deductions and raise rates by over 4 percentage points (0.11 times 39.6%). For the top statutory rate the effect would be to raise the effective rate of 35.2% to 39.6%.

Because of the significant trade-off between the number of tax filers subject to a flat-cap and revenue-raising potential, this option might have limited ability to broaden the base and could increase EMTRs for some tax filers. In any case where current deductions are greater than the cap, any current reduction in EMTR due to the deductions, in their current form, would be eliminated. If the flat-cap is set at relatively low levels, these increases in effective tax rates at the margin could appear across a wide range of incomes. If a flat-cap is designed to largely avoid increasing EMTRs on returns with an AGI less than $250,000, the cap would probably raise relatively little revenue (see Table 5) because it would retain a large non-marginal benefit for itemized deductions from a smaller pool of higher-income tax filers.

Share of AGI Cap on Itemized Deductions

A percentage of income cap on all itemized deduction claims could be used to limit the marginal tax rate effect to a smaller number of tax filers. For example, with an average deduction that is 9% of income at the margin, a percentage of income limit that is that high would, on average, not affect marginal rates for that individual.

A possible difficulty with this approach is that the constraint would be more binding on those with an AGI less than $250,000 where total itemized deduction claims are a higher share of income (see Table 2). It would, therefore shift a larger share of the burden of the tax increase to those below $250,000 as compared to a dollar limit. One possibility is to allow both a dollar ceiling and a percentage of income ceiling, and the tax filer can take the higher of the ceilings.

If the policy goal is to target higher-income tax filers, an alternative could involve placing percentage of income ceiling on those itemized deductions whose claims as a share of income rises at the higher-end of the income distribution. These provisions primarily include deductions for state and local income taxes and charitable gifts. For example, a 6% limit on these combined provisions would raise some revenue from tax filers with an AGI over $1 million while permitting most of the deductions to be taken by others (see Table 2). This proposal would still limit the increase in effective tax rates for those affected to about 11/2 percentage points on average (the difference between 10% and 5% multiplied by 39.6%). For the top rate, with 11% of deductions, the rate rises by the difference between 6% and 11%, multiplied by 39.6%, for 2 percentage points.

Limiting the Value of Certain Tax Expenditures

Like other broad proposals to restrict itemized deductions, limiting the value of certain tax expenditures (including some itemized deductions) could increase EMTRs. For example, if deductions effective at the margin are 11% of income for a tax filer facing a top marginal statutory tax rate of 39.6%, then limiting the value of itemized deductions reduces the EMTR by 4 percentage points, or to 35.6%, on average. Limiting itemized deductions to 2% of income produces a rate of 37.6% because the provision reduces taxes by 2% of income at the margin. Thus the EMTR rises by 2 percentage points compared to tax policy without the limit.

Limiting the Rate at which Itemized Deductions Could be Valued

President Obama's proposal to limit the tax rate at which itemized deductions could be valued to 28% would only affect tax filers in the top two tax brackets. Based on the analysis presented here, it could increase the top EMTR by 1.3 percentage point for those tax filers facing the top income tax rate of 39.6% (deductions of 11% at the margin times the difference between 39.6% and 28%, 0.11 times 0.116). However, this approach might be limited in its ability to raise revenue, as indicated in Table 5. This option would likely raise some revenue from itemized deductions that are not marginal.

Substituting a Credit for a Deduction

The policy option of substituting a credit for a deduction has a similar effect to the proposal to limit the rate at which deductions could be valued. In the case of a 28% credit, the effects would be the same as President Obama's proposal, although the credit would be available to non-itemizers unless it could be taken only if the standard deduction is not. For a 15% credit, more tax filers who currently itemize would encounter marginal effects. In the case of the top rate illustration, the increase in EMTR would be the difference between the rates (39.6% minus 15%) multiplied by the share of deductions (11%).

Conclusion: Issues of Effective Marginal Tax Rates

As indicated above, each of the potential approaches examined in this report could result in increases in EMTRs and some options have a limited ability to target the effects of restrictions on itemized tax deductions solely to higher-income tax filers. In these cases, policy goals aimed at raising revenue from higher-income tax filers may be harder to achieve. On the other hand, approaches that are more targeted and less likely to induce marginal tax rates have more limited potential to raise revenue.

To take one example, if all itemized deductions are eliminated, the top, statutory income tax rate would rise by around 4.4 percentage points. If an across-the-board percentage reduction in tax rates were adopted, the statutory rate could fall by 4.2 percentage points. If the across-the-board reduction in statutory tax rates is revenue neutral within income classes, the top rate reduction might be 5 percentage points at the top (as discussed in the subsequent section on distributional issues). In either case the effects are largely offsetting. For the high tax rate individuals, the tradeoff would be less favorable if dollar caps were used, because that change would raise less revenue but still have the same marginal effects.

Some of the economic analysis of the effects of restricting itemized deductions as a means to broaden the tax base to offset the revenue loss from cuts in statutory tax rates could be overlooking the effects of possible proposals on EMTRs. As discussed above, analysis of EMTRs could provide better estimates of effects on labor supply and savings, and hence economic growth, contrary to the practice of some studies.[59] Given the recent interest in using dynamic scoring in preparing cost estimates, as expressed in the Senate budget resolution (S.Con.Res. 8), the understanding of EMTRs as contrasted with statutory marginal tax rates is important if such a proposal becomes law (and if marginal tax rates affect certain types of behavior).[60] For example, in the tradeoff between ending itemized deductions at the top for a 5 percentage point rate reduction, and a net reduction of effective marginal tax rate of 0.6 percentage points, an estimate that used the statutory rate reduction would produce behavioral effects that are more than 8 times as large as they should be (5/0.6)

Even if a proposal could lead to higher effective marginal tax rates for some tax filers, however, this issue could be of limited importance since most evidence suggests these marginal effects on labor supply and saving behavior are relatively small.[61] Nevertheless, the analysis suggests that tax reform undertaken for the purpose of lowering statutory rates, rather than addressing the particular economic effects of the tax subsidized activities, may not accomplish its purpose.

BEHAVIORAL EFFECTS AND ALLOCATIVE EFFICIENCY

This section of the report turns to the more traditional arguments for base broadening, namely the specific merits of particular tax provisions. Presumably, a provision would be eliminated or revised for efficiency reasons if the behavior is undesirable, or if the subsidy to a desirable behavior is too large.

This discussion does not address the itemized deductions not classified as tax expenditures or the medical expense deduction, because the primary purpose of many of these provisions is to enhance vertical equity in the federal income tax code, as discussed above. In each of the other cases, both the merits of providing an incentive and the effectiveness of doing so are addressed. This section provides summaries. More detailed information and supporting references can be found in other CRS reports.[62]

Owner-Occupied Housing: Mortgage Interest and Real Property Tax Deductions

Homeownership is sometimes presumed to be a desirable social policy goal. Economists, however, generally justify subsidies on the grounds of economic efficiency, such as the case where there is too little owner-occupied housing because individuals do not do not take into account social benefits to home ownership in making their choices. Even in the presence of a large base of literature discussing the benefits and costs of homeownership, the literature has not come to a definitive conclusion on the merits of subsidizing homeownership.[63]

There are several positive, social benefits to homeownership, some of which result in spillover benefits (positive externalities) to other individuals in the community. Some view homeownership as benefiting communities because homeowners are thought to be more stable, maintain property better, and may be more involved citizens regarding community decisions. Homeownership can also provide a "nest egg" for retirement and is an important asset, especially of moderate income families. Economists, however, could justify subsidies on the grounds of economic efficiency if there was a market failure for homeownership. For example, there could be an undersupply of housing because private participants in the market may not be able to adequately capture the social value of the spillover benefits of homeownership.

At the same time, homeownership can also have negative effects. Homeowners may join in adopting exclusionary policies (such as large lot sizes) that restrict the supply of housing, or they may discriminate against certain groups. Homeowners could also oppose the growth of certain types of businesses in their communities, thereby limiting local sources of job creation. The concentration of assets in a home could lead to diminished diversity and increased exposure to risk in an individual's personal financial portfolio. Finally, households that cannot easily sell their home (for whatever reason) contribute to labor immobility which can cause burdens for society, such as more claims for unemployment benefits.[64]

Overall, the magnitude of these effects has been difficult to estimate. But, they do lead to some questions about the desirability of providing such large benefits for homeownership.

With regard to the home mortgage interest and real estate property tax deductions, there are two potential effects that could be of concern to policymakers. First, they could increase the rates of homeownership and increase the average size of homes. According to empirical research on the issue, it is the tenure choice (i.e., renting versus owning), rather than the size of homes, that is more likely to lead to positive externalities in a community. Evidence, however, suggests that tenure choice is not affected very much by the tax benefits. Historically, the rate of homeownership has not changed although changes in inflation and tax rates have significantly affected the relative cost of owning versus renting. Also, homeownership rates are high in many countries without these benefits. Those on the margin between choosing to rent or own are likely to be younger or have lower incomes, and thus are less likely to itemize their deductions. Finally, the major barrier to owning a home is saving enough to provide a down payment, an issue that is not affected by the tax subsidy. The mortgage interest deduction and property tax deduction (as well as the exclusion of imputed net rent) may, instead, provide additional incentives for individuals who already intend to choose owning over renting to spend more on housing than they would absent the tax deduction.[65]

Some proposals for restricting the deductions related to homeownership would target them more towards moderate-income individuals. These policies could include caps, limits on the value of deductions, or eliminating the benefit for secondary residences (e.g., vacation homes). Table 6 provides revenue estimates for some of these options. The current home equity loan deduction is not targeted towards a particular behavior because home equity funds can be used to finance spending unrelated to the home. Instead of these tax incentives, a more desirable alternative for some could be loan programs that make it possible for younger families to acquire homes.

The mortgage interest deduction and deduction of real property taxes are not the only provisions that reduce the cost of acquiring and maintaining a home. Economists argue that owner-occupied housing is also subsidized by the exclusion of net imputed rental income. Imagine two homeowners renting their houses to each other: they would include the rent received in income but deduct the homeownership costs, including depreciation, insurance, and maintenance as well as mortgage interest and property taxes. Thus, rather than claiming just deductions for mortgage interest and property taxes they would also increase their respective incomes by the net rental income. In other words, even if the deductions for home mortgage interest and real property taxes were eliminated, there would still be some tax benefits in place for homeowners. Moreover, eliminating deductions for home mortgage interest could put lower-income tax filers at a comparative disadvantage, as other individuals could have sufficient assets (such as higher-income tax filers) to offset the loss of tax benefits from the deduction by paying off their mortgages. Those that can pay off their mortgages effectively retain tax exemption because earnings on these assets have fallen; their net income may be no different, since they pay less interest, but also receive less capital income.

Charitable Deductions

Tax benefits for charity probably enjoy more support among economists because charitable contributions are subject to market failures due to "free-rider" problems. The free-rider issues in the charitable sector of the economy refer to the extent that contributions are often undersupplied because individual tax filers can benefit from the contributions of others (even if they do not contribute, themselves), thus giving some individuals an incentive not to contribute while still receiving the benefits of charitable activities.[66] For example, transfers to enhance public health can provide a social benefit to donors and also to non-donors if there is a social value to non-recipients, such reduced risk of contracting illness.

Two issues, however, could make the deduction questionable. The first issue is that an individual contributor could give less to charity than the revenue loss associated with their tax deduction claim. If this were the case, then government could provide more funds for charitable purposes through grants rather than a tax deduction. This effect occurs when the elasticity of charitable contributions (percentage change in charity contributions from a 1% change in tax rates) is less than one, which most current research shows.[67] In other words, the low elasticity found in this research indicates that changes in charitable contributions are not very responsive to changes in tax rates. The second issue is that the contributors may receive direct benefits, implicit benefits, or their contributions may go to charities that much of the population does not benefit from. For example, contributors could receive fringe benefits, such as front-row seats at the orchestra or box seats at sporting events, or may give to individual universities and art museums. In contrast, less than 8% of charitable contributions, by some estimates, goes directly to aid those in poverty.[68]

Adding a floor to the deduction for charitable contributions is often discussed as one option for reform. A floor that permitted only large contributions relative to income, could increase the tax-induced charitable contributions per dollar of revenue loss. For example, Table 6 provides revenue estimates for three different floor options (2% of income, $500, and $1,000) for the deduction for charitable contributions. A floor could also increase tax compliance since small donations would no longer be eligible. According to the latest data available, about 14% of contributions would no longer have a marginal incentive with a 2% floor, although the revenue gain would be 37% of the total tax expenditure.[69] The relatively larger gain in revenue compared with the reduction in incentive is because most of the value of the contributions are made by tax filers who would retain a marginal incentive to give even after disallowing contributions up to 2% of income. These individuals are more likely to be higher-income individuals.

As discussed subsequently in the section on administrative and transitional issues, some options related to the deduction for charitable contributions (including the floor and also limits on gifts of property) are also aimed at increasing tax compliance.

State and Local Income and Personal Property Tax Deductions

Deductions for state and local taxes reduce the costs to state and local governments of imposing taxes, and they could be viewed by some as a federal subsidy to the states. This implicit subsidy to the states could encourage more taxes or government services at the state and local level, or provide incentives for some states and localities to favor federally deductible taxes in their choice of revenue sources.

This assessment could lead some to question whether the federal taxpayers should subsidize activities in specific states or localities, whether via tax subsidies or via direct grants. Some government services provided by state and local governments do potentially benefit all federal taxpayers to some degree (e.g., roads) while others do not (e.g., residential waste management). Given the mobility of the population, there are some general benefits to educational services (which is also a recipient of some of the tax benefits of general obligation tax-exempt bonds). Similarly, taxpayers in one state or locality could benefit from the awareness that the poor are being cared for in another state or locality. Still, the overall spending of state and local governments tends to largely benefit their own residents. Moreover, federal tax deductions for state and local taxes are not targeted, particularly with regard to ability to pay federal income taxes. In addition, those states that have higher-income tax rates tend to also have a preference for higher levels of public goods so that taxpayers are receiving higher levels of public goods (that are exempt from income tax). Also, the fact that several states do not have income taxes creates an inequality in the benefits of federal tax deductions that vary depending on the mix of revenue sources.

Even if there is consensus among policymakers that the rationale of a federal tax subsidy for state and local governments is justified, alternatives to the current policy could still fulfill this rationale while also meeting other policy goals associated with federal tax reform. Depending on the primary policy goal, the deduction for state and local taxes could be capped at a flat-dollar or share of income, replaced with a credit, or certain types of state and local taxes could be disallowed. Table 6 provides revenue estimates for some of these options.

Distributional Effects

Economists generally approach distributional issues of tax policy through terms of vertical equity (how the tax change is distributed across income classes) and horizontal equity (the extent to which itemized deductions and changes in them might decrease or increase fairness across taxpayers similarly situated). The following section of the report analyzes various options to restrict itemized deductions from these two standards of economic equity.

Vertical Equity

Vertical equity is important to analyze because it affects how rates can be reduced if pursuing a policy that is neutral from a distributional as well as a revenue perspective. If base-broadening is primarily to raise revenue, it indicates which income groups are paying additional taxes. Some have proposed to have more revenue raised from higher income classes.

Although itemized deductions tend to benefit higher-income groups because they have more income, are more likely to itemize, and have higher tax rates, the relative concentration of tax benefits from itemized deduction differs across different provisions.[70] According to the estimates in Table 9, the share of tax benefits in 2012 from certain itemized deductions classified as tax expenditures for tax filers with incomes above $200,000 (the highest income range in Table 9) is 58% for charitable contributions and 56% for state and local taxes other than real estate. In contrast, those same tax filers receive 33% of the share of total tax benefits tax filers derived from the mortgage interest deduction and 25% share of the total tax benefits derived from the deduction for real estate taxes.

Part of the reason some of the tax benefits of certain itemized deductions are concentrated in higher-income levels is because much of the income at that level is concentrated among a smaller number of tax filers. The distribution of tax benefits relative to incomes can also be illustrated visually using concentration curves, as shown in Figure 1. The horizontal, x-axis of the concentration curve measures the cumulative percentage of income from poorest to richest. For example, the first 15% of cumulative adjusted gross income is the income reported by the poorest 50% of taxpayers in the sample. The vertical, y-axis measures the cumulative percentage of tax benefits of a tax expenditure. If the concentration is above the 45-degree diagonal line in the figures, then the tax benefits are larger as a share of income for lower-income taxpayers. If the concentration is below the diagonal line, then the tax benefits tend to accrue to high-income taxpayers (i.e., distributed more regressively).

Note that the tax benefits for home mortgage interest, property taxes, charitable contributions and state and local sales or income taxes are each distributed regressively. The deduction for medical expenses is the only provision that exhibits some form of progressivity.

Table 9. Distribution of Tax Benefits for Certain Itemized Deductions Classified as Tax Expenditures, 2012 (in millions of dollars)

Income[a]	Home Mortgage Interest	State and Local Taxes Other Than Real Estate	Real Estate Taxes	Charitable Contributions
$0-$10k	$1	[*][b]	[*]	[*]
$10k-$20k	$48	$5	$19	$9
$20k-$30k	$235	$39	$72	$67
$30k-$40k	$585	$126	$196	$185
$40k-$50k	$1,151	$303	$428	$397
$50k-$75k	$5,906	$1,927	$2,232	$2,014
$75k-$100k	$7,567	$3,027	$3,094	$2,727
$100k-$200k	$29,068	$14,262	$12,199	$10,581
+$200k	$23,606	$24,135	$6,071	$21,597
All	$68,166	$43,826	$24,310	$37,578

Source: U.S. Congress, Joint Committee on Taxation, *Estimates of Federal Tax Expenditures for Fiscal Years 2012- 2017*, committee print, 113th Cong., 1st sess., February 1, 2013, JCS-1-13, pp. 42-48.

[a] The income concept used to place tax returns into classes is adjusted gross income ("AGI") plus: (a) tax-exempt interest, (b) employer contributions for health plans and life insurance, (c) employer share of FICA tax, (d) workers' (e) nontaxable Social Security benefits, (f) insurance value of Medicare benefits, alternative minimum tax preference items, and (h) excluded income of U.S. citizens living abroad.

[b] [*] indicates a positive tax expenditure (i.e., net revenue loss) of less than $500,000.

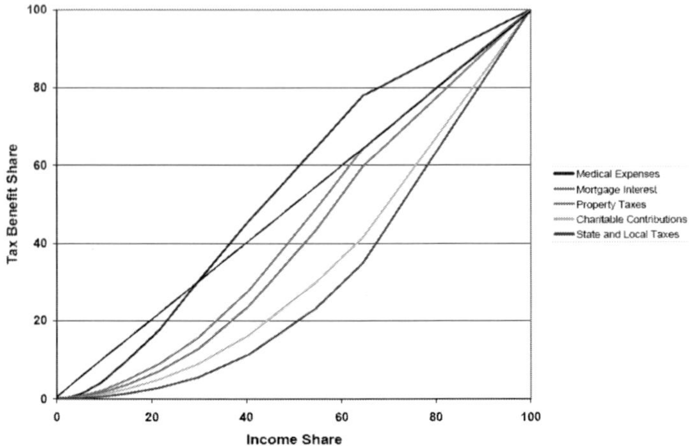

Source: CRS analysis of 2006 IRS Statistics of Income Public Use File. Reproduced from CRS Report R42435, *The Challenge of Individual Income Tax Reform: An Economic Analysis of Tax Base Broadening*, by Jane G. Gravelle and Thomas L. Hungerford.

Notes: The horizontal, x-axis of the concentration curve measures the cumulative percentage of income from poorest to richest. For example, the first 15% of cumulative adjusted gross income is the income reported by the poorest 50% of taxpayers in the sample. The vertical, y-axis measures the cumulative percentage of tax benefits of a tax expenditure. If the concentration is above the 45-degree diagonal line in the figures, then the tax benefits tend to accrue to lower-income taxpayers. If the concentration is below the diagonal line, then the tax benefits tend to accrue to high-income taxpayers.

Figure 1. Distribution of Tax Benefit and Income Share, Itemized Deductions.

Table 10 shows estimates from the Tax Policy Center (TPC) that provide a measure of progressivity by examining the tax benefits of certain itemized deductions as a share of a tax filer's after-tax income. If tax benefits are larger as a percentage of income for higher income individuals, then the provision is making after-tax income more unequal. TPC's data do not separate out real estate taxes, so the progressivity of state and local tax deductions reflects both the less progressive real estate taxes along with the more progressive income taxes and personal property taxes.

In general, the effects of certain itemized deductions on after-tax income are relatively small for tax units with an income less than $50,000. The benefits of the mortgage interest deduction rise through the middle and upper classes, but eventually fall until they become negligible. On the other hand, the tax benefits as a share of income for the deductions for charitable gifts and state and local taxes rise with income.

Table 10. Benefits of Deductions by Income Class, 2015

Cash Incomea	Share of All Tax Units	Share of Cash Income	Benefit as a Percentage of After-Tax Income		
			Mortgage Interest Deduction	Charitable Gift Deduction	State and Local Tax Deduction
$0-$10k	8.6%	0.6%	0.0%	0.0%	0.0%
$10k-$20k	14.2%	2.8%	0.0%	0.0%	0.0%
$20k-$30k	11.9%	3.9%	0.1%	0.0%	0.0%
$30k-$40k	11.1%	5.2%	0.2%	0.1%	0.1%
$40k-$50k	9.1%	5.4%	0.4%	0.1%	0.2%
$50k-$75k	16.8%	13.6%	0.7%	0.2%	0.4%
$75k-$100k	9.7%	11.2%	1.0%	0.3%	0.7%
$100k-$200k	13.6%	23.6%	1.4%	0.5%	1.2%
$200k-$500k	3.7%	13.5%	1.5%	0.8%	1.4%
$500k-$1m	0.5%	4.9%	0.9%	1.0%	1.9%
+$1m	0.4%	15.9%	0.1%	1.4%	2.2%
Total	100.0%	100.0%	0.8%	0.5%	1.0%

Source: Tax Policy Center, Tables T13-0076, 0078, and 0094, at http://taxpolicycenter.org/numbers/displayatab.cfm?template=simulation&SimID=466&relTTN=T13-0078.

[a] Cash income includes wages and salaries, employee contribution to tax-deferred retirement savings plans, business income or loss, farm income or loss, Schedule E income, interest income, taxable dividends, realized net capital gains, social security benefits received, unemployment compensation, energy assistance, Temporary Assistance for Needy Families (TANF), worker's compensation, veteran's benefits, supplemental security income, child support, disability benefits, taxable IRA distributions, total pension income, alimony received, and other income including foreign earned income. Cash income also includes imputed corporate income tax liability and the employer's share of payroll taxes. This puts the income measure on a pretax basis. Cash income is adjusted gross income (AGI) minus taxable state and local tax refunds, plus total deductions from AGI (IRA deductions, Student loan interest deduction, alimony paid, one-half of self-employment tax, moving expenses, penalty on early withdrawal of savings, self-employed health insurance deduction and medical savings account deduction, Keogh and self-employed SEP and SIMPLE plans), nontaxable pension income, tax-exempt interest, non-taxable social security benefits, cash transfers, worker's compensation, employee's contribution to tax deferred retirement savings plans, employer's share of payroll taxes and corporate tax liability. See Tax Policy Center, "Income Breaks for Distribution Tables," March 18, 2004, at http://www.taxpolicycenter.org/numbers/displayatab.cfm?DocID=574.

The percentage increase in after-tax income as a result of certain itemized deductions can help to inform the general number of percentage points that statutory tax rates could be cut to obtain a revenue-neutral, base-broadening restriction on itemized deductions. At the $500,000 and over income level, approximately where the top, marginal statutory tax rate begins, rates could be cut: approximately 1.75 percentage points if the itemized deduction for charitable gifts were eliminated, almost 3 percentage points if the deduction for state and local tax deductions were eliminated, and about 1.2 percentage points if the deduction for mortgage interest were eliminated.[71] Overall, the top statutory rate could be reduced by about 5 percentage points in a revenue-neutral manner if all three of these itemized deduction provisions were eliminated. Table 11 shows the effects of various across-the-board options to restrict itemized deductions for the three highest income classes (i.e., over $200,000). For tax units in these higher-income classes, a flat-cap of $50,000 could eliminate most of the increase in after-tax income as a result of itemizing. By comparison, limiting the value to 2% of income would eliminate part of the tax benefits of itemized deductions to tax units at the highest income levels. In terms of statutory rate reductions, the $50,000 flat-cap option could permit reductions of slightly over 4 percentage points, and the limit in value to 2% of income could allow a rate reduction of 3 percentage points.

Table 11. Effect on Certain Across-the-Board Restrictions on Itemized Deductions on Higher-Income Taxpayers, 2013

	Percentage Decrease in After-Tax Income		
Cash Income[a]	Eliminating All Itemized Deductions	$50,000 Flat-Cap on Deductions	Limit Value of Deductions to 2% of Income
$200k-$500k	3.0%	0.6%	2.3%
$500k-$1m	3.5%	1.3%	1.6%
+$1m	3.9%	3.9%	2.4%

Sources: Tax Policy Center (TPC), Table T13-0098, T12-0342, and T12-0358 at http://taxpolicycenter.org/ numbers/listdocs.cfm?BrowseTPC=true.

[a] See notes in Table 10 for a description of TPC's methodology for calculating "cash income."

Horizontal Equity

Whereas vertical equity considers the treatment of individuals with different income and presumably tax filers with different abilities to pay, horizontal equity considers taxpayers who have similar abilities to pay but different circumstances. Many features of the tax code recognize that factors other than income (e.g., family size, health, and age) affect ability to pay income taxes.

Certain itemized deductions are viewed by some as introducing horizontal inequities. For example taxpayers who own their homes have a lower effective tax burden than renters—even if both taxpayers have the same AGI. As another example, taxpayers with a preference for charitable donations have lower tax burdens than those with other preferences.

On the other hand, some itemized deductions could increase equity across taxpayers with similar abilities to pay. For example, a family with extraordinary medical expenses has a lesser ability to pay taxes than a family without those costs. A homeowner who has financed more of their home with assets will be effectively exempt from the income those assets are earning. By this logic, allowing a mortgage interest deduction may lead to more equitable treatment between those with a larger share of their home financed by a mortgage versus those with a lower share of their home financed by a mortgage. One could argue, however, the mortgage deduction also discriminates between homeowners and renters. In the context of eliminating the deduction for state and local taxes, a taxpayer who lives in a high tax state may pay more in federal taxes if state taxes are not deductible. Whether that treatment is equitable across taxpayers depends on whether the benefits from federal spending by the state are commensurate with taxes.

ADMINISTRATIVE AND TRANSITIONAL ISSUES

Reforms vary in the degree to which they will simplify tax administration by the government and compliance among tax filers. An outright repeal of itemized deductions, or a repeal of particular deductions, would tend to simplify both tax filing and compliance by reducing record-keeping and auditing for those deductions and reducing the general determination of whether a tax filer should choose to itemize their deductions or claim the standard deduction.[72] Some particular reforms might also simplify tax compliance and administration. For example, applying a floor to charitable deductions could eliminate the need for record-keeping for small donations that might also be less likely to be documented. Limits on contributions of property, such as household goods and clothing, could also reduce administrative costs because these items are hard to value and monitor.

Limiting the deduction for appreciated assets to basis could improve the valuation of assets by encouraging taxpayers to sell assets and donate the proceeds.

On the other hand, some approaches could add complications to tax compliance, by requiring additional computations. The proposal to limit the value of deductions, such as the President's proposal or FFM, could be particularly complicated for some tax filers as it could require computing tax liabilities under multiple additional scenarios, and perhaps re-computing the alternative minimum tax (AMT), depending on what or if modifications are made to that provision.[73] Current rules, for example, may require three tax calculations for high-income taxpayers, the basic, an adjustment for dividends and capital gains, and for the AMT. The FFM proposal would require a separate computation to compare tax liability income, with and without deductions, to determine the limit on tax benefits, and these might also have to be coordinated with capital gains and dividends calculations, as well as the AMT. In addition, calculations compared with the standard deduction would have to be made, because it is less obvious which is better. One question that could be asked is whether producing a tax code in which tax liability may need to be calculated as many as eight different ways a desirable step in tax reform?

Although these tax computation problems could be minor with the use of tax preparation software, they still could complicate choices for individuals who prepare their own returns without software. Moreover, any type of aggregate ceiling or floor would complicate year-to-year decisions about charitable contributions, which are the most easily adjusted in the short run. Other complications may arise relating to charitable contributions. For example, in the case of revisions to the treatment of donated property, individuals wishing to donate property may now need to sell that property. These additional transactions may add complexity for them, although it may relieve the charities of that burden. Floors and ceilings could lead to shifting charitable contributions across tax years to minimize effects.

In addition to administrative issues, there are also transitional issues. These issues are probably the most serious in the case of mortgage interest deductions, in which taxpayers entered into mortgages under the assumption of tax deductibility. Especially in the case of middle-income taxpayers, the presence and size of a mortgage is quite variable and may not be offset for many taxpayers with a rate reduction if mortgages are entirely eliminated. That is, since both itemizers and non-itemizers will face the same rates, tax burdens for current itemizers will rise even if the tax reform is distributionally neutral. Two solutions to these issues are to grandfather existing mortgages and only disallow the deduction of interest on new mortgages or to slowly lower the cap on mortgages over time. A second transitional issue, relating to owner occupied housing, is the potential short-run effect on an already troubled housing market. The solution might be slowly phasing down the caps.

APPENDIX A. HISTORY OF AND DETAILED DATA ON ITEMIZED DEDUCTIONS

A Concise History of Itemized Deductions

Itemized deductions have existed in some form since the creation of the first, permanent, U.S. income tax code in 1913. Tax filers have been able to itemize their deductions since the Revenue Act of 1913 (P.L. 63-16), which created the first permanent federal income tax. Deductions for interest paid or unexpected casualty losses were early provisions in the federal income tax code because many businesses were sole proprietorships (i.e., pass-through entities) in which the owner was personally liable for the costs of doing business.

Tax deductions expanded during the post-World War II period between 1947 and the end of the 1970s. Itemized deductions were created for state and local taxes, certain forms of interest, charitable contributions, extraordinary health expenses, and miscellaneous expenses. As a share of personal income, these deductions grew from approximately3.7% in 1947 to 10% in 1969, and then leveled off slightly to 9% in 1979.[74] Some say that the growth of these itemized deductions was dampened, in part, due to increases in the standard deduction amount. The standard deduction, which was formerly based on a share of income instead of a set amount adjusted for inflation, grew from a postwar low of 2.4% of income in 1969 to 6.5% of income by 1979.[75] This growth in the standard deduction reduced incentives for tax filers to itemize, because the value of the standard deduction exceeded the sum of their itemized deductions.

The Tax Reform Act of 1986 (TRA86) represented one of the most comprehensive tax code changes since the creation of the modern tax code in 1913. Among its main objectives, TRA86 sought to "broaden the base" of the individual income tax system, or expand the tax base without raising statutory tax rates, in a way that would provide an equitable distribution of tax reductions among individuals.[76] With regard to the individual income tax code,

TRA86 included reductions in marginal tax rates, reductions in the number of tax brackets, increase in the standard deduction, and the elimination or reformation of a variety of itemized deductions.

Within this policy framework, TRA86 eliminated some tax deductions and reformed other deductions that were left in the tax code. Deductions for state and local sales taxes were eliminated and numerous other deductions (e.g., employee business expenses, travel, and entertainment, and unreimbursed medical expenses) were limited either through higher thresholds or partial disallowance.[77] For example, TRA86 applied restrictions on the dollar amount of the home mortgage that was eligible for interest deduction ($1 million for married filing jointly/$500,000 for married filing separately), and limited the deduction only to a primary or secondary residence.[78]

Following TRA86, itemized deductions claims decreased in value by about one-quarter, dropping from 11.4% of personal income in 1985 to 9.2% by 1988. However, this decline in itemized deductions was partially offset in the tax base by a rise in the amount of tax filers claiming the standard deduction, whose value increased with the enactment of the TRA86.[79]

Since TRA86, Congress has authorized new itemized deductions. These individual provisions have been regularly reauthorized as part of a package of temporary "tax extenders" and are still in-effect under current law.[80] For example, an option to deduct state and local sales taxes *in lieu* of state income taxes was enacted in 2004.[81] In addition, qualified home mortgage insurance premiums became eligible for itemized deduction in 2007.[82]

Detailed Data on the Types of Itemized Deductions

This section of the report presents data tables of how many tax filers claimed specific itemized deductions on their tax returns, and what amount they claimed for each itemized deduction. These data come from the most recent version of the Internal Revenue Service's (IRS) Statistics of Income for 2010. In the aggregate, more than 46.6 million tax filers itemized their tax deductions (rather than claim the standard deduction) for a total of more than $1.2 trillion in claim amounts.[83]

Table A-1 and **Table A-2** disaggregate the number of tax returns and the claim amounts, respectively, for itemized deductions that are classified as tax expenditures. **Table A-3** and **Table A-4** disaggregate the number of tax returns and the claim amounts, respectively, for itemized deductions that are *not* classified as tax expenditures.

Table A- 1. Total Returns Claiming Itemized Deductions Classified as Tax Expenditures, 2010 (amounts are in thousands)

		Certain Taxes Paid			Homeownership			
Adjusted Gross Income (AGI)	Medical and Dental Expenses	State and Local Sales or Income	Real Estate	Personal Property	Mortgage Interest	Mortgage Points	Qualified Mortgage Insurance Premiums	Charitable Gifts
$0 under $20k	1,998	2,643	2,318	805	1,757	94	184	1,937
$20k under $50k	3,734	9,726	8,286	3,633	7,452	385	1,383	7,492
$50k under $100k	3,535	16,768	15,391	6,681	14,209	984	2,378	14,188
$100k under $200k	1,048	11,657	11,117	4,810	10,258	1,018	248	10,668
$200k under $250k	58	1,432	1,358	504	1,206	155	[*]	1,344
$250k under $500k	51	1,846	1,750	565	1,502	199	[*]	1,748
$500k under $1m	4	522	498	135	395	55	[*]	499
$1m under $5m	1	243	232	50	162	20	[*]	235
$5m +	[*]	28	27	5	14	1	[*]	27
Total[b]	10,431	44,869	40,982	17,191	36,957	2,916	4,197	38,143

Source: Internal Revenue Service (IRS), Statistics of Income 2010 – Table 3, Returns with Itemized Deductions, at http://www.irs.gov/uac/SOI—Individual-Statistical-Tables-by-Size-of-Adjusted-Gross-Income.

[a] [*] denotes that fewer than 1,000 tax filers in that particular AGI range claimed the deduction in 2010. The qualified mortgage premium is phased out for high incomes.

[b] Total tax filers were compiled from the totals listed in the original IRS data and might not equal the total tax filers displayed for a particular deduction in this table.

Table A-2.Total Claim Amounts for Itemized Deductions Classified as Tax Expenditures, 2010 (amounts are in millions)

		Certain Taxes Paid			Homeownership			
Adjusted Gross Income (AGI)	Medical and Dental Expenses	State and Local Sales or Income	Real Estate	Personal Property	Mortgage Interest	Mortgage Points	Qualified Mortgage Insurance Premiums	Charitable Gifts
$0 under $20k	$17,490	$2,006	$6,784	$270	$13,867	$51	$247	$3,243
$20k Under$50k	$27,391	$14,443	$22,966	$1,137	$58,053	$222	$1,646	$16,770
$50k under $100k	$26,526	$51,727	$50,246	$2,373	$130,469	$441	$3,497	$39,926
$100k under$200k	$10,758	$72,689	$53,022	$2,220	$125,351	$514	$216	$41,222
$200k under$250k	$1,215	$16,237	$9,508	$268	$20,206	$99	$1	$7,987
$250k under$500k	$1,527	$32,666	$15,897	$347	$30,462	$132	[*]a	$15,117
$500k under$1m	$305	$20,238	$6,893	$112	$10,238	$43	[*]	$9,398
$1m under$5m	$116	$27,460	$5,310	$59	$4,818	$18	[*]	$13,449
$5m +	$3	$25,227	$1,570	$15	$490	$2	[*]	$23,120
Total[b]	$85,336	$262,697	$172,201	$6,806	$393,957	$1,525	$5,609	$170,235

Source: Internal Revenue Service (IRS), Statistics of Income 2010 – Table 3, Returns with Itemized Deductions, at http://www.irs.gov/uac/SOI—Individual-Statistical-Tables-by-Size-of-Adjusted-Gross-Income.

[a] [*] denotes that total claims were less than $1,000,000 in that particular AGI range claimed the deduction in 2010. The qualified mortgage premium is phased out for high incomes.

[b] Total claim amounts were compiled from the totals listed in the original IRS data and might not equal the total claim amounts displayed for a particular deduction in this table.

Table A-3. Total Returns Claiming Itemized Deductions Not Classified as Tax Expenditures, 2010 (amounts are in thousands)

				Certain Limited Deductionsb			Unlimited Deductions	
Adjusted Gross Income (AGI)	Investment Interest Expenses	Other Taxes[a]	Casualty or Theft Losses	Employee Expenses	Tax Preparation Expenses	Other Misc.	Gambling Losses	Other Misc.[c]
$0 under $20k	72	263	12	370	1,197	1,968	43	20
$20k under $50k	140	1,020	35	3,144	4,561	7,401	187	113
$50k under $100k	305	1,944	29	6,198	8,580	13,532	314	132
$100k under $200k	413	1,581	23	4,114	6,127	9,795	314	115
$200k under $250k	108	238	2	368	765	1,232	244	20
$250k under $500k	245	340	1	350	842	1,710	30	48
$500k under $1m	124	106	0	66	228	564	48	29
$1m under $5m	95	56	[*][d]	18	103	321	7	31
$5m +	17	6	[*]	1	11	46	[*]	8
Total[e]	1,523	5,558	104	14,632	22,459	36,572	889	519

Source: Internal Revenue Service (IRS), Statistics of Income 2010 – Table 3, Returns with Itemized Deductions, at http://www.irs.gov/uac/SOI—Individual-Statistical-Tables-by-Size-of-Adjusted-Gross-Income.

[a] This category includes eligible deductions, such as foreign income taxes paid. See IRS "Topic 503 – Deductible Taxes," at http://www.irs.gov/taxtopics/tc503.html.

[b] Includes itemized deductions subject to the 2% of AGI floor and other limits. See IRS, "Publication 529 – Main Content," at http://www.irs.gov/publications/p529/ar02.html#en_US_2012_publink100026911.

[c] For a list of these unlimited itemized deductions, see IRS, "Publication 529 – Main Content," at http://www.irs.gov/publications/p529/ar02.html#en_US_2012_publink100027002.

[d] [*] denotes that fewer than 1,000 tax filers in that particular AGI range claimed the deduction in 2010.

[e] Total tax filers were compiled from the totals listed in the original IRS data and might not equal the total tax filers displayed for a particular deduction in this table.

Table A-4.Total Claim Amounts for Itemized Deductions Not Classified as Tax Expenditures, 2010 (amounts are in millions)

				Certain Limited Deductionsb			Unlimited Deductions	
Adjusted Gross Income (AGI)	Investment Interest Expenses	Other Taxes[a]	Casualty or Theft Losses	Employee Expenses	Tax Preparation Expenses	Other Misc.	Gambling Losses	Other Misc.[c]
$0 under$20k	$132	$159	$50	$1,594	$320	$3,739	$245	$81
$20k under $50k	$233	$464	$484	$16,540	$987	$23,675	$1,366	$525
$50k under $100k	$530	$952	$4,506	$28,776	$1,957	$41,542	$2,539	$434.4
$100k under $200k	$864	$928	$2,546	$19,474	$1,727	$32,672	$2,878	$636
$200k under $250k	$460	$156	$246	$2,239	$335	$5,420	$847	$125
$250k under $500k	$1,542	$309	$263	$2,291	$650	$9,863	$2,324	$463
$500k under $1m	$1,686	$135	$68	$654	$356	$6,883	$1,839	$292
$1m under $5m	$3,202	$183	$33	$348	$359	$10,965	$2,658	$325
$5m +	$4,965	$102	$4	$58,674	$161	$11,886	$1,402	$263
Totald	$13,619	$3,392	$2,234	$72,143	$6,857	$146,649	$16,101	$3,148

Source: Internal Revenue Service (IRS), Statistics of Income 2010 – Table 3, Returns with Itemized Deductions, at http://www.irs.gov/uac/SOI—Individual-Statistical-Tables-by-Size-of-Adjusted-Gross-Income.

[a] This category includes eligible deductions, such as foreign income taxes paid. See IRS "Topic 503 – Deductible Taxes," at http://www.irs.gov/taxtopics/tc503.html.

[b] Includes itemized deductions subject to the 2% of AGI floor and other limits. See IRS, "Publication 529 – Main Content," at http://www. irs.gov/publications/p529/ar02.html#en_US_2012_publink100026911.[c] For a list of these unlimited itemized deductions, see IRS, "Publication 529 – Main Content," at http://www.irs.gov/publications/p529/ar02.html#en_US_ 2012_publink100027002.

[d] Total claim amounts were compiled from the totals listed in the original IRS data and might not equal the total claim amounts displayed for a particular deduction in this table.

End Notes

[1] Office of Management and Budget, Fiscal Year 2014 - Budget of the U.S. Government, April 2013, p. 36, at http://www.whitehouse.gov/sites/default/files/omb/budget /fy2014/assets

[2] Senator Max Baucus and Representative Dave Camp, "Tax Reform Is Very Much Alive and Doable," *Wall Street Journal*, April 7, 2013, at http://online.wsj.com/article/SB100014 24127887323611604578396790773598474.html.

[3] See CRS Report R42435, *The Challenge of Individual Income Tax Reform: An Economic Analysis of Tax Base Broadening*, by Jane G. Gravelle and Thomas L. Hungerford, for a discussion and categorization of individual income tax expenditures.

[4] For example, see House Ways and Means Committee Chairman Dave Camp (MI), "Camp Announces Hearing on Tax Reform and Tax Provisions Affecting State and Local Governments," March 19, 2013, at http://waysandmeans.house.gov/calendar/eventsingle.aspx?EventID=323582; House Ways and Means Committee Chairman Dave Camp (MI), "Camp Announces Hearing on Tax Reform and Charitable Contributions," February 14, 2013, at http://waysandmeans.house.gov/calendar/eventsingle.aspx?EventID=319000; and House Ways and Means Committee Chairman Dave Camp (MI), "Camp Announces Hearing on Tax Reform and Residential Real Estate," April 25, 2013, at http:// waysandmeans.house.gov/calendar/eventsingle.aspx?EventID=330283.

[5] CRS Report R43012, *Itemized Tax Deductions for Individuals: Data Analysis*, by Sean Lowry.

[6] For more information on how tax deductions reduce taxable income, see CRS Report R42872, *Tax Deductions for Individuals: A Summary*, by Sean Lowry.

[7] Although this choice is generally the case, the Government Accountability Office (GAO) estimated that about 510,000 tax filers (who account for about 0.1% of all individual taxes paid) in 1998 overpaid their taxes by claiming the standard deduction, even though they could have itemized their deductions for a greater tax benefit. GAO did not determine the reasons why tax filers might have done this. See U.S. General Accounting Office, *Tax Deductions: Further Estimates of Taxpayers Who May Have Overpaid Federal Taxes by Not Itemizing*, GAO-02-509, March 2002, at http://www.gao.gov/new.items/d02509.pdf.

[8] See CRS Report R43012, *Itemized Tax Deductions for Individuals: Data Analysis*, by Sean Lowry, for data on itemizers.

[9] P.L. 93-344, Section 3(3).

[10] Joint Committee on Taxation, Estimates Of Federal Tax Expenditures For Fiscal Years 2012-2017, JCS-1-13, February 1, 2013, at https://www.jct.gov/publications.html?func= startdown&id=4504.For a discussion on the measurement of tax expenditures, see CRS Report RL34622, *Tax Expenditures and the Federal Budget*, by Thomas L. Hungerford; and Jane G. Gravelle, "Tax Expenditures," in *The Encyclopedia of Taxation and Tax Policy*, ed. Joseph J. Cordes, Robert D. Ebel, and Jane G. Gravelle (Washington, DC: The Urban Institute Press, 2000), pp. 379-280.

[11] Not always is there a consensus for what provisions are considered as tax expenditures. For example, in the Analytical Perspectives to the President's FY2014 Budget Proposal, the itemized deduction for casualty losses is listed as a tax expenditure whereas JCT does not. See Office of Management and Budget, Analytical Perspectives, Fiscal Year 2014 - Budget of the U.S. Government, April 2013, p. 246, at http://www.whitehouse.gov/sites/default /files/omb/ budget/fy2014/assets/spec.pdf.

[12] See CRS Report R41796, *Deficit Reduction: The Economic and Tax Revenue Effects of the Personal Exemption Phaseout (PEP) and the Limitation on Itemized Deductions (Pease)*, by Thomas L. Hungerford, for more information.

[13] This floor was recently increased by health reform legislation; it was 7.5% for all taxpayers prior to 2013.

[14] The deductions not subject to the Pease limitation are medical and dental expenses, investment interest, qualified charitable contributions, and casualty and theft losses.

[15] See Martin A. Sullivan, "Deduction Caps: The Next AMT?," *Tax Notes*, December 10, 2012.

[16] U.S. Congress, Senate Committee on the Budget, *Tax Expenditures: Compendium of Background Material on Individual Provisions*, committee print, 112th Cong., 2nd sess., December 2012, S.Prt. 112-45 (Washington: GPO, 2012), pp. 5-6.

[17] For additional discussion of these issues, see CRS Report R42435, *The Challenge of Individual Income Tax Reform: An Economic Analysis of Tax Base Broadening*, by Jane G. Gravelle and Thomas L. Hungerford.

[18] Estimates of revenue come from CRS analysis of data from the Urban Brookings Tax Policy Center, Tables T13- 0099 at http://taxpolicycenter.org/numbers/listdocs.cfm? BrowseTPC=true. Data on deficits and revenues for FY2015 comes from CBO, The Budget and Economic and Outlook: Fiscal Years 2013-2023, February 5, 2013, at http://www.cbo.gov/publication/43907. It would be about a third of the baseline under a measure of current policy that maintained discretionary spending at real levels and continued the "doc fix" to keep Medicare payments to doctors from falling significantly.

[19] Martin Sullivan, "Deduction Caps Can Raise Marginal Rates, Cut Economic Growth," *Tax Notes*, November 26, 2012, pp. 939-943.

[20] For more discussion, see CRS Report R42111, *Tax Rates and Economic Growth*, by Jane G. Gravelle and Donald J. Marples.

[21] These and other data were obtained from Internal Revenue Service, Statistics of Income 2010, Individual Income Tax Returns with Itemized Deductions, at http://www.irs.gov/uac/SOI-—Individual-Statistical-Tables-bySize-of-Adjusted-Gross-Income.

[22] This number is the solution to x in the equation x+0.06*(1-x) = 0.41.

[23] The top 5% percent of the income distribution, with incomes of $230,000 or more, pays 53% of income taxes; the top 1% pays 33%. See Tax Policy Center, Table T11-0356 at http://www.taxpolicycenter.org/numbers/displayatab.cfm? DocID=3274.

[24] For example, reports indicate that Governor Mitt Romney proposed capping itemized deductions by a flat amount of $17,000 as one aspect of his tax policy platform during the 2012 presidential campaign. See Martin A. Sullivan, "Economic Analysis: A First Look at Romney's Deduction Cap," *Tax Notes*, October 15, 2012.

[25] However, nine states do not have an individual income tax. These states include Alaska, Florida, New Hampshire, Nevada, South Dakota, Tennessee, Texas, Washington, and Wyoming. See CRS Report RL32781, *Federal Deductibility of State and Local Taxes*, by Steven Maguire.

[26] For example, an itemizer in a 25% tax bracket that claims a $4,000 deduction in state and local income taxes owes $1,000 ($4,000*0.25) less in federal income taxes. In contrast, an itemizer in a 39.6% tax bracket that claims a $4,000 deduction in state and local income taxes owes $1,584 ($4,000*0.396) less in federal income taxes. Thus, the value of the same $4,000 deduction is $584 greater for the itemizer facing a top marginal tax rate of 39.6% than for the itemizer facing a top marginal tax rate of 25%.

[27] *Analytical Perspectives* FY 2014 Budget, at http://www.gpo.gov/fdsys/pkg/BUDGET-2014-PER/pdf/BUDGET2014-PER.pdf, p. 197.

[28] *Analytical Perspectives*, FY 2012 Budget, at http://www.gpo.gov/fdsys/pkg/BUDGET-2012-PER/pdf/BUDGET2012-PER.pdf, p. 212.

[29] Martin Feldstein, Daniel Feenberg, and Maya MacGuineas, *Capping Individual Tax Expenditure Benefits*, National Bureau of Economic Research, Working Paper 16921, April 2011, at http://papers.nber.org/papers/w16921. In their paper, the researchers estimate the effects of various levels of this limit, from 2% to 5% of AGI, but focus their analysis on the 2% limit. Martin Feldstein and Daniel Feenberg are associated with the National Bureau of Economic Research (NBER) and Maya MacGuineas is the President of the Committee for a Responsible Federal Budget.

[30] Martin Feldstein, "The Tax Hike Canard," *Foreign Affairs*, December 11, 2012.

[31] Committee for a Responsible Federal Budget (CRFB), *Raising Revenue from Higher Earners through Base Broadening*, Tax Working Paper, November 15, 2012, at http://crfb.org/sites/default/files/ raising_revenue_from_higher_earners_11_15-2.pdf..

[32] Ibid., p. 3.

[33] See ibid., p. 7 for the list of additional tax expenditures included under this updated version of the FFM option.

[34] This proposal could also be extended to apply to tax exclusions.

[35] Non-refundable credits can reduce an individual's tax liability to zero (but not below), whereas a refundable credit can reduce an individual's tax liability below zero and result in a refund check issued by the Internal Revenue Service.

[36] Harvey S. Rosen, *Public Finance*, 7th ed. (New York, NY: McGraw-Hill Irwin, 2005), pp. 376-377.

[37] This commission is often referred to as "Simpson-Bowles" because the chairs include former-Congressman Alan Simpson and former Clinton-White House Chief of Staff Erskine Bowles.

[38] The National Commission on Fiscal Responsibility and Reform, *The Moment of Truth*, December 2010, p. 31, at http://www.fiscalcommission.gov/sites/fiscalcommission.gov /files/documents/TheMomentofTruth12_1_2010.pdf. In the event that there is not enough support for a complete elimination of tax deductions, the commission recommended a "failsafe" option of an across-the-board reduction in itemized deductions.

[39] Simpson-Bowles would also limit the proposed tax credit for mortgage interest on the first $500,000 of mortgage debt on a primary residence (compared with the $1 million in mortgage debt across primary and second residences under permanent law for the current deduction) and not allow a credit for home equity interest (compared with the $100,000 deduction under permanent law for the current deduction).

[40] Alice Rivlin has been director of the Congressional Budget Office (CBO) and the Office of Management and Budget (OMB), and is currently a Senior Fellow in Economic Studies at the Brookings Institution. Pete Dominici was a U.S. Senator from New Mexico from 1973 to 2009. These proposals were part of both versions of the D-R proposal, first issued in November 2010 and revised in December 2012. See Senator Pete Domenici and Alice Rivlin, *Restoring America's Future*, Bipartisan Policy Center, November 2010, at http://bipartisanpolicy.org/sites/default/files/ BPC%20FINAL%20REPORT%20FOR%20PRINTER%2002%2028%2011.pdf, and Senator Pete Domenici and Alice Rivlin, *Domenici-Rivlin Debt Reduction Task Force Plan 2.0,* December 2012, at http://bipartisanpolicy.org/sites/ default/files/FINAL%20Domenici-Rivlin%202%200%20Plan.pdf.

[41] The Patient Protection and Affordable Care Act (P.L. 111-148, as amended) increased the floor for the deduction for extraordinary medical expenses from 7.5% of AGI to 10% of AGI for tax years 2013 and beyond; the higher limit will apply to those aged 65 and over in 2016.

[42] See CRS Report R41596, *The Mortgage Interest and Property Tax Deductions: Analysis and Options*, by Mark P. Keightley.

[43] See Congressional Budget Office, Reducing the Deficit: Spending and Revenue Options, March 2011, pp. 146-147, at http://www.cbo.gov/sites/default/files/cbofiles/ftpdocs /120xx/doc12085/03-10-reducingthedeficit.pdf.

[44] U.S. Congress, Senate Committee on the Budget, *Tax Expenditures: Compendium of Background Material on Individual Provisions*, committee print, prepared by the Congressional Research Service, 112th Cong., 2nd sess., December 2012, S. Prt. 112-45 (Washington: GPO, 2012), pp. 357-362; and Testimony of Eric J. Toder in U.S. Congress, House Committee on Ways and Means, *Options to Reform the Home Mortgage Interest Deduction*, Hearing on Tax Reform and Residential Real Estate, 113th Cong., 1st sess., April 25, 2013, p. 3, at http://waysandmeans.house.gov/uploadedfiles/toder_ testimony_ 42513_fc.pdf.

[45] See CRS Report RL32781, *Federal Deductibility of State and Local Taxes*, by Steven Maguire.

[46] In contrast to the pre-1986 law, state sales and use taxes can only be deducted *in lieu* of income taxes, not in addition to, under current law. See Appendix A for a concise history of itemized tax deductions, including the deduction for state and local taxes.

[47] See Internal Revenue Service Statistics of Income, Individual Income Tax Returns with Itemized Deductions, at http://www.irs.gov/uac/SOI—Individual-Statistical-Tables-by-Size-of-Adjusted-Gross-Income.

[48] See testimony of C. Eugene Steuerle before the Ways and Means Committee, on Tax Reform and Charitable Contributions, February 13, 2013, at http://waysandmeans.house.gov /uploadedfiles/steuerletestimony02.14.2013fc.pdf.

[49] Significant restrictions have already been placed on vehicles, by valuing the donation at the amount the charity actually receives for them on sale. See Internal Revenue Service Publication 4303, "A Donor's Guide to Car Donations," at http://www.irs.gov/pub/irs-tege/pub4303.pdf.

[50] Joint Committee on Taxation, *Options to Improve Tax Compliance and Reform Tax Expenditure*, JCS-02-05, January 27, 2005.

[51] These data are from 2005. See Deena Ackerman and Gerald Auten, "Tax Expenditures for Non-Cash Charitable Contributions," *National Tax Journal*, vol. 64, no. 2, part 2, June 2011, pp. 651-688.

[52] For information on the extension of this provision, see CRS Report R42894, *An Overview of the Tax Provisions in the American Taxpayer Relief Act of 2012* , by Margot L. Crandall-Hollick.

[53] See CRS Report RL34608, *Tax Issues Relating to Charitable Contributions and Organizations*, by Jane G. Gravelle and Molly F. Sherlock, for further discussion of charitable contributions.

[54] See testimony of C. Eugene Steuerle before the Ways and Means Committee, on Tax Reform and Charitable Contributions, February 13, 2013, at http://waysandmeans.house.gov /uploadedfiles/steuerletestimony02.14.2013fc.pdf.

[55] In mathematical terms, these calculations are conducted as follows: 39.6% (the statutory, marginal tax bracket) times 0.894 (representing the 10.6% across-the-board reduction in marginal statutory tax rates) = 4.2 (percentage point reduction in the 39.6% statutory tax rate); and 10% times 0.894 = 1.1.

[56] For the purposes of the FFM proposal, this logic also extends to provisions such as the exclusion for employer-provided health insurance.

[57] For more information on PPACA taxes scheduled to go into effect in 2013, see CRS Report R41128, *Health-Related Revenue Provisions in the Patient Protection and Affordable Care Act (ACA)*, by Janemarie Mulvey, specifically the section entitled "Provisions Affecting Individuals"; and CRS Report R41413, *The 3.8% Medicare Contribution Tax on Unearned Income, Including Real Estate Transactions*, by Mark P. Keightley.

[58] This illustration reflects in a general way what is seen in Table 2 and Table 7 for high-income taxpayers: large deductions for state and local income taxes and charity, small or negligible deductions for real estate and mortgage interest.

[59] For example, a study of the projected growth effects of Governor Mitt Romney's tax proposal during the 2012 presidential campaign that was widely cited used changes in *statutory* tax rates and therefore, would have exaggerated the proposal's effects on economic growth. For that matter, the proposal might have a contractionary effect on growth if provisions, such as dollar caps on tax benefits, were used as part of base-broadening reform, and these provisions led to the increase in effective marginal tax rates discussed through this report. See John W. Diamond, *The Economic Effects of the Romney Plan*, August 3, 1012, at http://bakerinstitute.org/publications/Diamond-RomneyTaxReformPlan080312.pdf. This study was also referenced in Harvey S. Rosen, "Growth, Distribution, and Tax Reform: Thoughts on the Romney Proposal," Princeton University, Griswold Center for Economic Policy Studies, Working Paper No. 228, September 2012, at http://www.princeton.edu/ceps /workingpapers/228rosen.pdf. Another analysis that relied on statutory rate reductions was Martin Feldstein, Romney's Tax Plan Can Raise Revenue," *Wall Street Journal*, August 28, 2012, at http://www.nber.org/feldstein/wsj08282012.pdf.

[60] Dynamic revenue estimation takes into account macroeconomic feedback effects from the economy. For more discussion on dynamic- versus static-revenue estimating, see CRS Report RS22020, *Dynamic Revenue Estimating: A Brief Overview*, by Jane G. Gravelle; and CRS Report RL31949, *Issues in Dynamic Revenue Estimating*, by Jane G. Gravelle.

[61] See CRS Report R42111, *Tax Rates and Economic Growth*, by Jane G. Gravelle and Donald J. Marples, for a review of the evidence.

[62] For a discussion that touches on all of them, see CRS Report R42435, *The Challenge of Individual Income Tax Reform: An Economic Analysis of Tax Base Broadening*, by Jane G. Gravelle and Thomas L. Hungerford.

[63] For a discussion of this literature, see CRS Report R41596, *The Mortgage Interest and Property Tax Deductions: Analysis and Options*, by Mark P. Keightley.

[64] Homeownership, in general, tends to be a barrier to relocating when job market conditions change because it involves transaction costs. Moreover, if housing prices decrease at the same time that the labor market deteriorates, homeowners may be even more reluctant (or unable) to sell because they may have a loss and perhaps have difficulty repaying the mortgage.

[65] Net imputed rental income is the estimated value of the net rental income a homeowner "pays" to himself, and, at the same time, avoids paying to someone else for a particular service.

[66] A more in-depth discussion of the economics of charitable giving can be found in CRS Report R40919, *An Overview of the Nonprofit and Charitable Sector*, by Molly F. Sherlock and Jane G. Gravelle.

[67] For a review of the literature, see CRS Report R40518, *Charitable Contributions: The Itemized Deduction Cap and Other FY2011 Budget Options*, by Jane G. Gravelle and Donald J. Marples.

[68] The share of giving that goes to charities serving basic needs accounted was about 7.5% of giving; if indirect giving to the poor (including in- kind benefits such as education and

health care that are part of the functions of other charities) is included, the amount is estimated at around 19% to 23% (depending on which estimate is used for the share of religious giving that goes to the poor). The share going to basic giving declines for higher incomes. See *Patterns of Household Charitable Giving by Income Group, 2005*, Prepared for Google by the Center on Philanthropy at Indiana University, summer 2007, at http://www.philanthropy.iupui.edu/files/research/giving_focused_on_meeting_needs_of_th e poor_july_2007.pdf.

[69] Based on the 2006 Statistics of Income public use file. In that year there were $175.7 billion in contributions, with $22.3 billion for taxpayers below the floor and $2.3 billion for taxpayers who switch to the standard deduction. These estimates were reported in CRS Report R42435, *The Challenge of Individual Income Tax Reform: An Economic Analysis of Tax Base Broadening*, by Jane G. Gravelle and Thomas L. Hungerford.

[70] Tax benefits for a tax filer are defined as their deduction claim multiplied by their top marginal tax rate.

[71] These calculations weigh the $500,000 to $1 million income classes as 28% of the total of the $500,000 and over class, and multiply by 1.36 to adjust for a third of taxable income in qualified dividends and capital gains, 15% of income deducted to reach taxable income and after tax income 76% of adjusted gross income. These distributional shares are based on data for 2010 in Internal Revenue Service, Statistics of Income, at http://www.irs.gov/uac/SOI-—Individual-Statistical-Tables-by-Size-of-Adjusted-Gross-Income.

[72] Even though a growing number of tax filers are using electronic tax filing resources that automatically determine whether the tax filer's potential itemized deductions exceed the standard deduction, many tax filers still complete their tax returns using paper forms.

[73] For an explanation of the AMT, see CRS Report RL30149, *The Alternative Minimum Tax for Individuals*, by Steven Maguire.

[74] C. Eugene Steuerle, *The Tax Decade: How Taxes Came to Dominate the Public Agenda* (Washington, DC: The Urban Institute Press, 1992), p. 18.

[75] Ibid.

[76] U.S. Congress, Joint Committee on Taxation, *General Explanation of the Tax Reform Act of 1986*, committee print, 100th Cong., 1st sess., May 4, 1687, JCS-10-87 (Washington: GPO, 1987).

[77] Alan J. Auerbach and Joel Slemrod, "The Economic Effects of the Tax Reform Act of 1986," *Journal of Economic Literature*, vol. 35, no. 2 (June 1997), p. 597.

[78] U.S. Congress, Senate Committee on the Budget, *Tax Expenditures: Compendium of Background Material on Individual Provisions*, committee print, prepared by the Congressional Research Service, 111th Cong., 2nd sess., December 2010, S.Prt. 111-58 (Washington: GPO, 2010), pp. 335-340.

[79] Jon Bakija and Eugene Steuerle, "Individual Income Taxation Since 1948," *National Tax Journal*, vol. 44, no. 4 (December 1991), p. 459.

[80] For the latest status of itemized deductions under current law, see CRS Report R42872, *Tax Deductions for Individuals: A Summary*, by Sean Lowry.

[81] The American Jobs Creation Act of 2004 (P.L. 108-357) initially enacted this provision for the 2004 and 2005 tax years. In contrast to the pre-1986 law, state sales and use taxes can only be deducted *in lieu* of income taxes, not in addition to.

[82] The Tax Relief and Health Care Act of 2006 (P.L. 109-432) initially enacted this provision for the 2007 tax year.

[83] Internal Revenue Service (IRS), Statistics of Income 2010 – Table 3, Returns with Itemized Deductions, at http://www.irs.gov/uac/SOI—Individual-Statistical-Tables-by-Size-of-Adjusted-Gross-Income.

In: Tax Deductions
Editor: Pierre Thibault

ISBN: 978-1-62808-491-7

Chapter 2

ITEMIZED TAX DEDUCTIONS FOR INDIVIDUALS: DATA ANALYSIS*

Sean Lowry

SUMMARY

Reforming or limiting itemized tax deductions for individuals has gained the interest of policymakers as one way to increase federal tax revenue, increase the share of taxes paid by higher-income tax filers, simplify the tax code, or reduce incentives that might lead to inefficient economic behavior. However, limits on deductions, in the views of some, would cause adverse economic effects or changes in the distributional burden of the federal income tax code. This report is intended to identify who claims itemized deductions, for how much, and for which provisions?

This report analyzes data to inform the policy debate about reforming itemized tax deductions for individuals. In 2010, 33% of all tax filers chose to itemize their deductions rather than claim the standard deduction. In addition, the data indicate that both the share of tax filers that itemize their deductions and the amount claimed by each tax filer as adjusted gross income (AGI) increases. AGI is the basic measure of income under the federal income tax and is the income measurement before itemized deductions and personal exemptions are taken into

* This is an edited, reformatted and augmented version of a Congressional Research Service publication, CRS Report for Congress R43012, prepared for Members and Committees of Congress, from www.crs.gov, dated March 21, 2013.

account. Although higher-income tax filers are more likely to itemize their deductions and claim a larger amount of itemized deductions than lower-income tax filers, the majority (65.8%) of itemizers in 2010 was composed of tax filers with an AGI less than $100,000, and 91.3% of itemizers had an AGI below $200,000.

Tax filers in different income ranges tend to claim different itemized deductions. In 2010, tax filers in higher income ranges claimed deductions for charitable gifts, state and local taxes, and real estate property taxes at higher rates than tax filers in lower income ranges. For example, the deduction for charitable gifts was claimed by 46% of tax filers with an AGI between $50,000 and $100,000, whereas it was claimed by 76% to 94% of tax filers with an AGI above $100,000. Deductions for state and local taxes and the deduction for charitable gifts comprise a larger share of itemized deductions as income rises.

The four largest itemized deductions are estimated to account for 17.8% ($195.7 billion) of the approximately $1.1 trillion in tax expenditures in FY2014. These deductions are for home mortgage interest, state and local taxes, charitable gifts, and real estate taxes.

These findings have several implications for policy options that would seek to reform or limit itemized tax deductions. First, efforts to target limits on itemized tax deductions toward higher-income tax filers are limited in the amount of revenue that can possibly be raised. Although higher-income tax filers claim a larger average amount of deductions, these tax filers make up a small share of itemizers.

Second, the structure of a limit on itemized deductions could affect which deductions a tax filer might claim. Although a limit based on a percentage reduction in the overall tax benefits of itemized deductions would not change the relative choice of deduction claims, limits based a flat-dollar value cap likely would alter deduction claims and possibly tax filer behavior. This could happen if a tax filer has deductions that exceed a flat-dollar value cap, because the tax filer must make a decision about which deductions to actually claim. Even if a tax filer cannot claim a tax deduction for a particular activity, the tax filer might still engage in the activity for other reasons (although possibly to a lesser extent).

Third, the structure of a limit on itemized deductions also has an effect on its ability to raise revenue. Limiting deductions might raise the taxable income of some individuals, thereby pushing them into a higher marginal tax bracket, and tax a higher share of their income at that higher marginal tax rate. However, certain combinations of deduction limits may shift some tax filers to claim the standard deduction instead of itemizing. In this case, the revenue increase by limiting itemized deduction would be partially offset by more tax filers claiming the standard deduction.

INTRODUCTION

Reforming or limiting itemized tax deductions for individuals has gained the interest of policymakers as one way to increase federal tax revenue, increase the share of taxes paid by higher-income tax filers, simplify the tax code, or reduce incentives that might lead to inefficient economic behavior. However, limits on deductions, in the views of some, would have adverse economic effects or changes in the distributional burden of the federal income tax code. Discussions about itemized tax deduction reform are informed by scrutiny of tax filer data.

This report analyzes the most recently available public data from the Internal Revenue Service's (IRS's) Statistics of Income (SOI) to provide an overview of who claims itemized deductions, what they claim them for, and the amount in deductions claimed. In addition, the revenue loss associated with several of the larger deductions is presented using data obtained from the Joint Committee on Taxation's (JCT) tax expenditure estimates. This report concludes with a brief discussion of the implications of various policy options to reform or limit itemized deductions. More in-depth discussion on options for reforming itemized tax deductions, as a whole or individually, can be found in other CRS reports.[1]

AN OVERVIEW OF ITEMIZED TAX DEDUCTIONS

Individual income tax filers have the option to claim either a standard deduction or the sum of their itemized deductions on the federal income tax Form 1040. The *standard deduction* is a fixed amount, based on filing status, available to all taxpayers. Alternatively, tax filers may claim *itemized deductions*.

Tax filers that itemize must list each item separately on their tax returns and be able to provide documentation in the event of an IRS audit that the expenditures have been made. Whichever deduction a tax filer claims—standard or itemized—the deduction amount is subtracted from adjusted gross income (AGI) in the process of determining taxable income.[2] AGI is the basic measure of income under the federal income tax and is the income measurement before itemized deductions and personal exemptions are taken into account.

Generally, only individuals with aggregate itemized deductions greater than the standard deduction find it worthwhile to itemize.[3] The tax benefit of choosing to itemize is the amount that their itemized deductions exceed the standard deduction multiplied by their top marginal income tax rate.

Some itemized deductions can only be claimed if they meet or exceed minimum threshold amounts (also known as a floor) to simplify tax administration and compliance. Floors usually come in the form of a limit based on a percentage of AGI. For example, eligible extraordinary medical and dental expenses must amount to 10% of AGI in order to claim an itemized deduction in 2013; total expenses less than this floor are not eligible for an itemized deduction.

In addition, some itemized deductions are subject to a cap (also known as a ceiling) in benefits or eligibility. Caps are meant to reduce the extent that tax provisions can distort economic behavior, limit revenue losses, or reduce the availability of the deduction to higher-income tax filers. For example, the itemized deduction for home mortgage interest can only be claimed for the value of interest payments made on the first $1 million of mortgage debt.

ANALYSIS OF TAX DATA

This section of the report uses publicly available tax data from the IRS to provide a profile of itemizers and some insight into trends among various itemized deduction provisions. Itemized deductions are often grouped together in broader discussions of tax policy, in part because they are grouped together on the tax Form 1040.[4]

But, itemized deductions exist for a variety of reasons and are designed in ways such that they target (or exclude) certain types of tax filers. Analysis of data on these deductions can inform these discussions over reforming one or more itemized deduction provisions. Specifically, the data analysis in this report intends to identify who claims itemized deductions, for how much, and for which provisions?

This analysis might be relevant to the 113th Congress, as there has been growing congressional interest in reforming or limiting itemized tax deductions for individuals. Some see reforming itemized tax deductions as one way to increase federal tax revenue (and possibly contribute to deficit reduction), increase the share of taxes paid by higher-income tax filers, simplify the tax code, or reduce incentives that might lead to inefficient economic behavior.

Who Claims Itemized Tax Deductions?

In 2010, 33% of all tax filers chose to itemize their deductions rather than claim the standard deduction.[5] Of this 33% of tax filers, a greater share of higher-income individuals chose to itemize their deductions compared with lower-income individuals. *Table 1* shows the share of tax filers that chose to itemize their deductions and the average sum of those deductions in 2010 by AGI.

Higher-income tax filers chose to itemize their deductions more often than lower-income tax filers in 2010. As shown in *Table 1*, the share of tax filers that chose to itemize in higher income ranges above $200,000 remained virtually the same, although the average sum of itemized deductions claimed increased substantially. For taxpayers with an AGI above $200,000, the share that itemized ranged from 95% to 97% and the average sum of itemized deductions claimed per itemizer ranged from $41,079 to $443,680. In contrast, 85% of tax filers with an AGI between $100,000 and $200,000 chose to itemize their deductions in 2010, with an average of $27,729 in deductions claimed. Six percent of tax filers with an AGI less than $20,000 chose to itemize their deductions in 2010, with an average of $15,432 in deductions claimed.

Table 1. Share of Tax Filers Claiming Itemized Tax Deductions and Average Deduction Claimed, by Adjusted Gross Income (AGI), 2010

Adjusted Gross Income	Number of Itemizers	Share of Tax Filers that Itemized	Average Sum of Itemized Deductions Claimed Per Itemizer
$0 to $20k	3,057,363	6%	$15,432
$20k to $50k	10,334,994	23%	$15,810
$50k to $100k	17,258,142	57%	$19,540
$100k to $200k	11,873,957	85%	$27,729
$200k to $250k	1,450,337	95%	$41,079
$250k to $500k	1,866,973	96%	$55,991
$500k to $1million	527,916	97%	$101,502
+$1million	274,826	98%	$443,680

Source: CRS analysis of the Internal Revenue Service's Statistics of Income 2010 Data, Table 3, at http://www.irs.gov/uac/SOI-Tax-Stats—Individual-Statistical-Tables-by-Size-of-Adjusted-Gross-Income.

What is the Value of an Itemized Tax Deduction?

Two key concepts are important in understanding the value of itemized deductions for tax filers: the progressive structure of the federal income tax and *statutory* versus *effective* tax rates. First, not all income is taxed at the same tax rate, at the federal level. As income increases through various ranges, or brackets, it is taxed at graduated rates. Second, the maximum statutory tax rate a tax filer faces is not necessarily the same as the actual, or effective, tax rate the tax filer pay on his or her income. Statutory tax rates are set in law, and form the basis of the progressive federal income tax structure. However, tax provisions that reduce taxable income (e.g., deductions and exemptions) might also reduce the tax filer's effective tax rate, if they are large enough to put the tax filer in a lower statutory marginal (top) tax rate. A simple calculation of the effective tax rate is the amount of taxes paid, or final tax liability, divided by gross adjusted income (AGI). For this reason, the effective tax rate is also often referred to as the average tax rate.

For example, an itemizer in a 25% tax bracket that claims a $4,000 deduction in state and local income taxes owes $1,000 ($4,000*0.25) less in federal income taxes, than if the tax filer did not claim the deduction. In other words, the value of any given itemized tax deduction is equal to the deduction amount claimed times a tax filer's statutory income tax rate. If the tax value of the deduction is large enough to put the tax filer into a different, lower tax bracket, then the value of the deduction could be less for the tax filer because a share of the income earned is taxed at a lower tax rate. For behavioral effects, however, it is the value of the last increment of deduction that is valued at the tax filer's marginal tax rate that is most likely capable of determining to what extent the individual participates in the behavior (or participates at all).

Although higher-income tax filers both tend to itemize at higher rates and claim a larger average total of itemized deductions, the majority of itemizers have incomes below $100,000. *Figure 1* shows the distribution, by AGI, of total itemizers and total itemized deduction claimed in 2010. The majority (65.8%) of itemizers in 2010 was composed of tax filers with an AGI less than $100,000, and 91.3% of itemizers had an AGI below $200,000.

Compared with the distribution of itemizers, the distribution of total itemized deduction claim values are more evenly distributed across income ranges. As shown in *Figure 1,* a majority (55%) of total itemized deductions claims were made by tax filers with an AGI greater than $100,000. Although tax filers with an AGI more than $1 million comprised 0.6% of itemizers they claimed 10.0% of all itemized tax deductions in 2010. Similarly, tax filers with an AGI between $500,000 and $1 million accounted for 1.1% of itemizers, but they claimed 4.4% of all itemized deduction. Tax filers with an AGI between $50,000 and $100,000 accounted for 37.0% of all itemizers, but they claimed 27.7% of all itemized deductions.

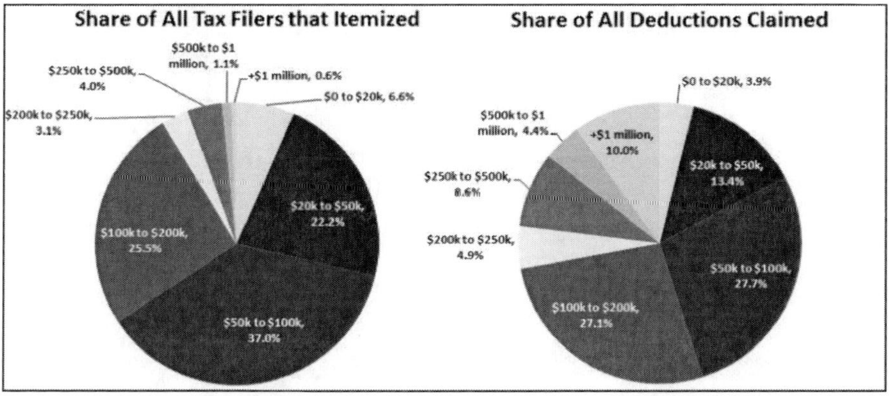

Source: CRS analysis of the Internal Revenue Service's Statistics of Income 2010 Data, Table 3, at http://www.irs.gov/uac/SOI-Tax-Stats—Individual-Statistical-Tables-by-Size-of-Adjusted-Gross-Income.

Figure 1. Shares of Tax Itemizers and Itemized Deductions Claimed, by Adjusted Gross Income (AGI), 2010.

Analysis of Selected Deductions

Another way to analyze tax data on itemized deductions is to look at selected deductions. By analyzing data on selected deductions, it becomes apparent that there is wide variation in who claims a specific itemized deduction. For example, selected deductions tend to benefit different types of itemizers, based on their income. In addition to differences in the income of the itemizer, the variation in itemized deduction claims can also be explained, in part, by the structure of certain provisions (e.g., floors or ceilings that are designed to limit claims).

Tax filers in different income ranges tend to claim different itemized deductions. *Table 2* shows the average amount claimed in 2010 for selected deductions and the share of total tax filers that itemized in each income class that claimed a particular deduction.[6] Tax filers in higher income ranges claimed deductions for charitable gifts, state and local taxes, and real estate property taxes at higher rates than tax filers in lower income ranges. For example, the deduction for charitable gifts was claimed by 46% of tax filers with an AGI between $50,000 and $100,000; 76% of tax filers with an AGI between $100,000 and $200,000; and more than 88% of tax filers with an AGI over $200,000. Fewer tax filers in the highest income group (with an AGI greater than $1 million) than in the $100,000-$1 million income groups claimed the home mortgage interest deduction, possibly due to a greater ability for some individuals to pay for home purchases with cash (i.e., they did not have a mortgage).[7]

Table 2. Average Amount Claimed by Tax Filers for Various Tax Deductions, 2010 (share of total tax filers in each income group claiming each itemized deduction)

Adjusted Gross Income (AGI)	Home Mortgage Interest	Charitable Gifts	State & Local Taxes	Real Estate Taxes	Medical Expenses	Unreimbursed Employee Business Expenses
$0 to	$7,891	$1,674	$759	$2,926	$8,754	$4,305
$20k	(4%)	(4%)	(5%)	(5%)	(4%)	(1%)
$20k to	$7,790	$2,238	$1,485	$2,771	$7,335	$5,261
$50k	(17%)	(17%)	(22%)	(19%)	(8%)	(7%)
$50k to	$9,182	$2,814	$3,085	$3,265	$7,502	$4,643
$100k	(47%)	(46%)	(55%)	(50%)	(12%)	(20%)
$100k to	$12,220	$3,864	$6,235	$4,769	$10,265	$4,734
$200k	(73%)	(76%)	(83%)	(79%)	(7%)	(29%)
$200k to	$16,747	$5,939	$11,339	$6,998	$20,846	$6,075
$250k	(79%)	(88%)	(93%)	(89%)	(4%)	(24%)
$250k to	$20,278	$8,645	$17,690	$9,081	$29,813	$6,547
$500k	(78%)	(90%)	(95%)	(90%)	(3%)	(18%)
$500k to	$25,900	$18,836	$38,711	$13,836	$67,669	$9,915
$1million	(73%)	(92%)	(96%)	(92%)	(1%)	(12%)
+$1million	$30,011	$138,997	$193,727	$26,471	$121,468	$27,858
	(63%)	(94%)	(97%)	(93%)	(<1%)	(7%)

Source: CRS analysis of the Internal Revenue Service's Statistics of Income 2010 Data, Tables 1.2 and 3, at http://www.irs.gov/uac/SOI—Individual-Statistical-Tables-by-Size-of-Adjusted-Gross-Income.

Notes: Claim amounts are as reported before limits were applied. See footnote 6.

Few tax filers, in general, claimed the deduction for extraordinary medical and dental expenses—particularly at the highest income ranges. The 7.5% of AGI floor required to claim the deduction in 2010 limited the amount of taxpayers that could be eligible for this provision.[8]

Average tax deduction values indicate which provisions have the largest effects in reducing different tax filers' taxable incomes. The deduction for state and local taxes was the largest average deduction amount claimed for any deduction by tax filers with an AGI above $500,000 (aside from the infrequent instance where a tax filer claimed the itemized deduction for extraordinary medical expenses). In contrast, the mortgage interest deduction was, on average, the largest single deduction, by amount, claimed by tax filers with an AGI less than $500,000 (aside from the medical expenses deduction). The average deduction for charitable gifts also increases sharply for tax filers with an AGI of $1 million or above. The average amount of the charitable gift deduction claimed by tax filers with an AGI between $500,000 and $1 million was $38,711. In contrast, the average amount of the charitable gift deduction for tax filers with an AGI more than $1 million was $193,727 in 2010.

Figure 2 shows the distribution of various deductions claimed across income groups. These data illustrate several trends.

- The home mortgage interest deduction made up the largest share of total itemized deduction claims for itemizers with an AGI between $20,000 and $250,000.
- The largest share of total itemized deduction claims for tax filers with an AGI more than $250,000 was composed of the deduction for state and local taxes.
- The deductions for state and local taxes and charitable contributions composed a larger share of total deductions claimed as income rise.

Table 3 shows the amounts claimed for certain itemized deductions as a share of the total income of itemizers. There was no general trend across income ranges, with respect to the shared of total itemized deductions claimed as a share of AGI. Among all income ranges, itemized deductions made up the largest share of AGI (approximately 17.5%) for itemizers with an AGI between $100,000 and $250,000. For itemizers with an AGI above $250,000, however, total itemized deductions tended to decline as a share of AGI. For example, itemized deductions made up 13.2% of the AGI reported by tax filers with an AGI of $1 million or more that itemize.

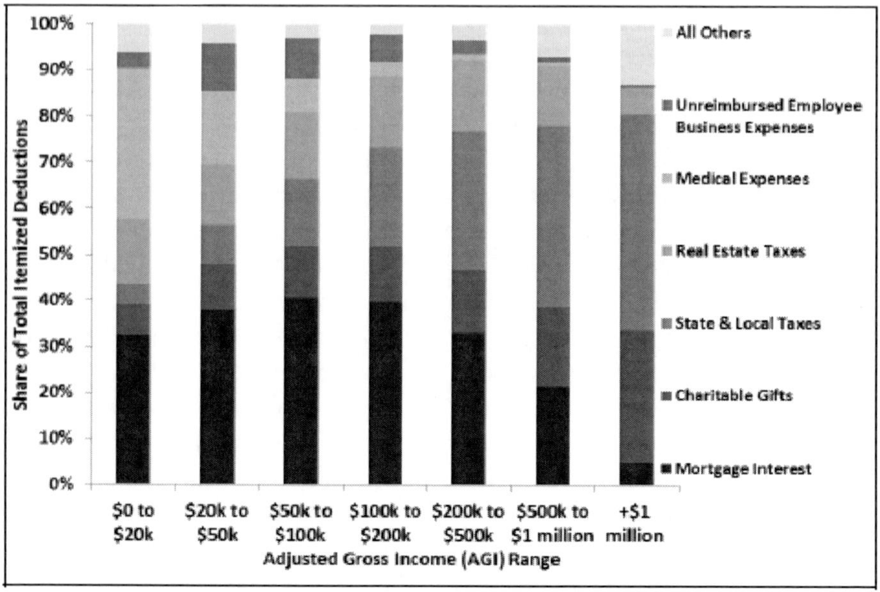

Source: CRS analysis of the Internal Revenue Service's Statistics of Income 2010 Data, Tables 1.2 and 3, at http://www.irs.gov/uac/SOI—Individual-Statistical-Tables-by-Size-of-Adjusted-Gross-Income.

Notes: Claim amounts are as reported before limits were applied. See footnote 6.

Figure 2. Distribution of Itemized Deductions Claimed, by Adjusted Gross Income (AGI), 2010.

Although the data presented in *Table 3* provide a different way to calculate the distribution of selected itemized deductions, the results largely resemble those in previous tables and figures. For example, the deduction for state and local taxes as well as the deduction for charitable gifts made up the largest share of income for itemizers with an AGI of $1 million or more.

WHICH ITEMIZED DEDUCTIONS CONTRIBUTE MOST TO REVENUE LOSS?

Some itemized deductions are classified as tax expenditures, or losses in federal tax revenue. Table 4 shows the Joint Committee on Taxation (JCT) estimates for the top five itemized deductions that are expected, under current law, to contribute most to annual tax expenditures in FY2014.

Table 3. Amount of Itemized Deductions Claimed as a Share of the Income of Itemizers, by Adjusted Gross Income (AGI), 2010

Adjusted Gross Income	Home Mortgage Interest	State & Local Taxes	Charitable Gifts	Real Estate Taxes	All Itemized Deductions
$0 to $20k	4.7%	1.1%	0.7%	2.3%	16.0%
$20k to $50k	3.9%	1.1%	1.0%	1.6%	11.1%
$50k to $100k	6.0%	1.8%	2.4%	2.3%	15.5%
$100k to $200k	6.7%	2.2%	3.9%	2.8%	17.6%
$200k to $250k	5.9%	2.3%	4.8%	2.8%	17.5%
$250k to $500k	4.7%	2.3%	5.1%	2.5%	16.2%
$500k to $1million	2.8%	2.6%	5.5%	1.9%	14.5%
+$1million	0.6%	4.0%	5.7%	0.7%	13.2%

Source: CRS analysis of the Internal Revenue Service's Statistics of Income 2010 Data, Tables 1.2 and 3, at http://www.irs.gov/uac/SOI—Individual-Statistical-Tables-by-Size-of-Adjusted-Gross-Income.

Notes: Claim amounts are as reported before limits were applied. See footnote 6.

Table 4. Itemized Tax Deductions Estimated to Contribute Most to Revenue Losses in FY2014

Deduction Provision	Tax Expenditure Estimate in FY2014, (in billions of dollars)	Share of All Individual Tax Expenditures in FY2014[a]
Mortgage Interest Deduction	$71.7	6.5%
State & Local Income or Sales Taxes	$51.8	4.7%
Charitable Gifts	$43.6	3.9%
Real Estate Taxes	$28.6	2.6%

Source: CRS analysis of Joint Committee on Taxation (JCT), Estimates of Federal Tax Expenditures, For Fiscal Years 2012-2017, 113th Congress, 1st session, February 1, 2013, JCS-1-13 (Washington: GPO, 2013).

[a] Based on the JCT publication, above, individual tax expenditures are estimated to be $1,109.3 billion and corporate tax expenditures are estimated to be $119.7 billion ($1,229 billion total) in FY2014. JCT does not provide a value for provisions that are estimated to be less than JCT's de-minimus amount of $50 million in revenue losses for FY2013 to FY2017. These calculations do not assume a change in tax filer behavior in response to interactive changes to one or more provisions.

Tax expenditures are defined under the Congressional Budget and Impoundment Control Act of 1974 (P.L. 93-344) as "revenue losses attributable to provisions of the Federal tax laws which allow a special exclusion, exemption, or deduction from gross income or which provide a special credit, a preferential rate of tax, or a deferral of tax liability."

The four itemized deductions that contribute most to tax expenditures in FY2014 are estimated to account for 17.8% ($195.7 billion) of the approximately $1.11 trillion in individual tax expenditures.[9] As shown in *Table 4,* the home mortgage interest deduction, which is estimated to account for 6.5% ($71.1 billion) of annual tax expenditures in FY2014, is the largest tax expenditure claimed by tax filers. The mortgage interest deduction is also the fourth largest individual tax expenditure overall.[10] The deduction for state and local taxes is estimated to account for 4.7% ($51.8 billion) of FY2014 tax expenditures, followed by charitable gifts (3.9%), and real estate taxes (2.6%).[11]

POLICY IMPLICATIONS

Congress might consider policies limiting itemized deductions.[12] Some view these limits as one way to increase federal revenue, increase the progressive structure of the federal income tax code, simplify the tax code, or reduce economic distortions in the tax code.[13] When a tax filer loses the ability to take deductions, then their taxable income increases (absent other behavioral changes). Others seek to limit itemized deductions to increase progressivity in the tax code, where tax filers with higher incomes pay a larger share of their income in taxes than those with less income.

Arguments against broad limits to itemized deductions vary. The economic effects of limiting itemized tax deductions might be undesirable for some. Those who are willing to accept the economic consequences of limits on itemized tax deductions might argue for reform of individual provisions, rather than broader limits, because the rationale for itemized deductions varies. For example, some might find the deduction for charitable contributions desirable but not the deduction for state and local income taxes.[14]

Others argue that higher-income tax filers already provide most of the revenue collected through the individual federal income tax, and might oppose further efforts to increase the progressivity of the federal income tax code. These concerns might arise because some high-income individuals are also small business owners, and higher taxation on their income (and, in turn, their business's profits), might have a negative effect on job creation.[15]

Some proposals to reform or limit itemized deductions include a flat, dollar-value cap on total deductions; a percentage limit on the value of deductions; converting deductions into credits, and various others.[16] Although this report does not assess these policies in depth, it does provides insights from the data analysis on itemized tax deductions that might be useful for informing the debate concerning reform options.

First, efforts to target limits on itemized tax deductions toward higher-income tax filers are restricted in the amount of revenue that can possibly be raised. During the 2012 presidential campaign, a flat-dollar value cap was suggested as one possible way to increase federal tax revenue. However, to avoid increasing the taxable income of most households, the dollar-value cap on total deductions would need to be set high enough that it will not be lower than the average deduction values for those in the middle or lower portion of the income distribution of tax filers. For example, *Table 1* suggests that a flat-cap of $25,000 would affect the average itemizer with an AGI above $100,000. However, estimates show that higher caps have more limited ability to raise revenue.[17] As *Figure 1* and *Table 1* show, there are fewer itemizers at top of the income distribution.

Second, the form of a limit on itemized deductions might affect which deductions a tax filer might claim. If a tax filer potentially has deductions that exceed a flat-dollar value cap, then the tax filer must choose which deductions to actually claim. *Table 2* provides some estimates of which deductions may "fill" up a taxpayer's cap, if that cap is based on a flat dollar amount, whereas *Table 3* provides estimates under a limit in the form of a share of AGI.

A reduction in the tax benefits derived from activities eligible for tax deduction can possibly affect tax filer behavior. Deductible activities that are more easily adjustable in the short run (e.g., charitable giving) could be reduced after enactment of a limit on deductions in order to claim deductions from activities that are more difficult to adjust or plan for in the short-run (e.g., state and local taxes, or extraordinary medical expenses).[18] Over time, tax filers might adjust their behavior to accommodate for limits in itemized deductions (e.g., renting a residence might be more preferable for some, if they can no longer deduct the interest costs of their mortgage). However, a tax filer might still engage in particular activities for other reasons (although possibly to a lesser extent) even if the tax filer no longer can obtain a tax benefit from doing so.[19] *Figure 2* shows what share of a tax filer's itemized deductions are composed of tax-deductible behaviors that are relatively more difficult to adjust in the short run versus behaviors that are relatively easier to adjust in the short run.

In contrast, limits that are not tied to fixed, dollar-values could be structured in a way that does not cause a tradeoff in choosing which tax-deductible activity to claim. For example, these limits could be capped based on a share of the tax filer's income. Although these limits would be less likely to cause a tradeoff between tax-deductible activities, they may reduce the tax-beneficial value of these activities. By reducing the value of those activities (in terms of tax liability), a tax filer might choose to claim a smaller value of deductions related to a certain activity (based on the behavioral response for each activity).

Third, the extent to which a limit on itemized deductions increases revenue depends on its structure. Limits on itemized deductions increase the amount of income of itemizers that is subject to taxation, thereby increasing revenue. Limiting deductions might raise the taxable income of some individuals, thereby pushing them into a higher marginal tax bracket, and tax a higher share of their income at a higher marginal tax rate.[20] Certain combinations of deduction limits may shift some tax filers to claim the standard deduction instead of itemizing. In this case, the revenue increase by limiting itemized deduction would be partially offset by more tax filers claiming the standard deduction.

End Notes

[1] For example, see CRS Report R42435, The Challenge of Individual Income Tax Reform: An Economic Analysis of Tax Base Broadening, by Jane G. Gravelle and Thomas L. Hungerford.

[2] For more information on how tax deductions reduce taxable income, see CRS Report R42872, Tax Deductions for Individuals: A Summary, by Sean Lowry.

[3] Although this is generally the case, the Government Accountability Office (GAO) estimated that about 510,000 tax filers (representing about 0.1% of all individual taxes paid) in 1998 overpaid their taxes by claiming the standard deduction, even though they could have itemized their deductions for a greater tax benefit. GAO did not determine the reasons why tax filers might have done this. See U.S. General Accounting Office, Tax Deductions: Further Estimates of Taxpayers Who May Have Overpaid Federal Taxes by Not Itemizing, GAO-02-509, March 2002, at http://www.gao.gov/new.items/d02509.pdf.

[4] This report analyzes 2010 data, which are the most recently available public data from the IRS.

[5] CRS analysis of the Internal Revenue Service's Statistics of Income 2010 Data, Table 1.2, at http://www.irs.gov/uac/ SOI-Tax-Stats—Individual-Statistical-Tables-by-Size-of-Adjusted-Gross-Income.

[6] All reported claim amounts in this report are tallied before limits were applied. In 2010, a deduction for medical expenses must have been in excess of 7.5% of AGI. A deduction for unreimbursed employee business expenses, when combined with all other "miscellaneous deductions," must have been in excess of 2% of AGI.

[7] In addition, the deduction for home mortgage interest is limited to interest on the first $1 million of mortgage debt. For more information on the home mortgage interest deduction, see CRS Report R41596, The Mortgage Interest and Property Tax Deductions: Analysis and Options, by Mark P. Keightley. On the other hand, higher-income individuals might prefer taking a mortgage out on their house rather than paying in cash if they believe that they can invest the money that they would otherwise use to pay their house off at a higher rate of return than the cost of the interest on the mortgage.

[8] The floor required to claim the deduction for extraordinary medical and dental expenses is 10% of AGI for tax years 2013 and beyond. See CRS Report R42872, Tax Deductions for Individuals: A Summary, by Sean Lowry.

[9] These calculations do not assume a change in tax filer behavior in response to interactive changes to one or more provisions. For example, elimination of the top five largest tax expenditures could lead to an estimated revenue gain in FY2014 of less than $208.1 billion because some taxpayers might claim the standardized deduction rather than itemize their deductions.

[10] The largest individual tax expenditure overall is the exclusion of employer contributions for health care, health insurance premiums, and long-term care insurance premiums at $143.0 billion for FY2014. See Joint Committee on Taxation (JCT), Estimates of Federal Tax Expenditures, For Fiscal Years 2012-2017, 113th Cong., 1st sess., February 1, 2013, JCS-1-13 (Washington: GPO, 2013).

[11] See Table 4.

[12] There is an income-triggered "limitation" on the value of itemized deductions (called "Pease," after Rep. Donald Pease who initially sponsored the legislative provision) for tax years 2013 and beyond. For tax filers affected by Pease, the total of certain itemized deductions is reduced by 3% of the amount of AGI exceeding the threshold. The total reduction, however, cannot be greater than 80% of the deductions. However, the Pease limit is triggered by income, not amount of deductions claimed, and is effectively an additive tax rate rather than a limit on itemized deductions. For more information, see CRS Report R42872, Tax Deductions for Individuals: A Summary, by Sean Lowry.

[13] Some say that itemized deductions should be limited because they distort economic behavior, by providing individuals with tax incentives to engage in activities that would otherwise be viewed as inefficient.

[14] However, eliminating deductions for one type of activity but not another might lead to unequal treatment of similar activities. For an example of how this might relate to deductions for charitable giving and the deduction for state and local taxes (SALT), see Martin A. Sullivan, "Economic Analysis: Why the SALT Deduction Is Always Under Attack," Tax Notes, December 17, 2012.

[15] For more information, see CRS Report R41392, Small Business and the Expiration of the 2001 Tax Rate Reductions: Economic Issues, by Jane G. Gravelle and Sean Lowry. The authors of this report estimate that between 2%-3% of small businesses were subject to the top marginal income tax rates in 2012.

[16] For a sample of policy options to limit itemized deductions, see Tax Policy Center (TPC), "Options to Repeal or Limit Itemized Deductions," at http://www.taxpolicycenter.org/taxtopics/Limit-Itemized-Deductions.cfm; Office of Management and Budget, Fiscal

Year 2013 Budget of the U.S. Government, p.39, at http://www.whitehouse.gov/sites/default/files/omb/budget/fy2013/assets/budget.pdf; Martin Feldstein, Daniel Feenberg, and Maya MacGuineas, Capping Individual Tax Expenditure Benefits, National Bureau of Economic Research, Working Paper 16921, April 2011, at http://papers.nber.org/papers/w16921.

[17] Prior to the permanent changes in marginal tax rates in the American Taxpayer Relief Act of 2012 (ATRA; P.L. 112- 240), the TPC estimated a cap of $25,000 could raise between $1.18 trillion and $1.3 trillion in revenue over 10 years, relative to a current law baseline and current policy baseline, respectively. In contrast, TPC estimated that a flat-cap of $50,000 could raise between $727 billion and $749 billion in revenue over 10 years. See Tax Policy Center, "T12- 0273—Options to Repeal or Limit Itemized Deductions; Impact on Tax Revenue, 2013-2022," October 17, 2012, at http://www.taxpolicycenter.org/taxtopics/Limit-Itemized-Deductions.cfm.

[18] See Martin A. Sullivan, "Deduction Caps: The Next AMT?," Tax Notes, December 10, 2012.

[19] For example, some researchers argue that charitable gifts result in "consumption" benefits or "warm glow" for the giver, such as social recognition and personal satisfaction. Those tax filers that are more motivated by these consumption benefits might be less responsive to changes in tax preferences for charitable giving. See Roger Colinvaux, Brian Galle, and Eugene Steuerle, Evaluating the Charitable Deduction and Proposed Reforms, Urban Institute, June 2012, p. 9, at http://www.urban.org/UploadedPDF/412586-Evaluating-the-Charitable-Deduction-andProposed-Reforms.pdf. For analysis and estimates of the behavioral responses of charitable giving to itemized deduction caps, see CRS Report R40518, Charitable Contributions: The Itemized Deduction Cap and Other FY2011 Budget Options, by Jane G. Gravelle and Donald J. Marples.

[20] The effect of limiting (or repeal) of certain tax deductions on revenue would depend on how a proposal is structured. For more information see Leonard E. Burman, Christopher Geissler, and Eric J. Toder, "How Big Are Total Individual Tax Expenditures, and Who Benefits From Them," American Economic Review, Papers and Proceedings of the One Hundred Twentieth Annual Meeting of the American Economic Association, vol. 98, no. 2 (May 2008), pp. 79-83.

In: Tax Deductions
Editor: Pierre Thibault
ISBN: 978-1-62808-491-7

Chapter 3

TAX DEDUCTIONS FOR INDIVIDUALS: A SUMMARY*

Sean Lowry

SUMMARY

Every tax filer has the option to claim deductions when filing their income tax return. Deductions serve four main purposes in the tax code: (1) to account for large, unusual, and necessary personal expenditures, such as extraordinary medical expenses; (2) to encourage certain types of activities, such as homeownership and charitable contributions; (3) to ease the burden of taxes paid to state and local governments; and (4) to adjust for the expenses of earning income, such as unreimbursed employee expenses.

Some tax deductions can be taken by individuals even if they do not itemize. These deductions are commonly referred to as above-the-line deductions, because they reduce a tax filer's adjusted gross income (AGI, or the line). In contrast, itemized and standard deductions are referred to as below-the-line deductions, because they are applied after AGI is calculated to arrive at taxable income.

Tax filers have the option to claim either a standard deduction or to itemize certain deductions. The standard deduction, which is based on filing status, is, among other things, intended to reduce the complexity of paying taxes, as it requires no additional documentation. Alternatively,

* This is an edited, reformatted and augmented version of Congressional Research Service, Publication No. R42872, dated February 5, 2013.

tax filers claiming itemized deductions must list each item separately on their tax return and be able to provide documentation that the expenditures being deducted have been made. Only tax filers with deductions that can be itemized in excess of the standard deduction find it worthwhile to itemize. Whichever deduction the tax filer claims—standard or itemized—the amount is subtracted from AGI.

Deductions differ from other tax provisions that can reduce a tax filer's final tax liability. Deductions reduce final tax liability by a percentage of the amount deducted, because deductions are calculated before applicable marginal income tax rates. In contrast, tax credits generally reduce an individual's tax liability directly, on a dollar-for-dollar basis, because they are incorporated into tax calculations after marginal tax rates are applied.

Some deductions can only be claimed if they meet or exceed minimum threshold amounts (usually a certain percentage of AGI) in order to simplify tax administration and compliance. In addition, some deductions are subject to a cap (also known as a *ceiling*) in benefits or eligibility. Caps are meant to reduce the extent that tax provisions can distort economic behavior, limit revenue losses, or reduce the availability of the deduction to higher-income tax filers.

Because some tax filers and policymakers may not have detailed knowledge of tax deductions, this report first describes what they are, how they vary in their effects on reducing taxable income, and how they differ from other provisions (e.g., exclusions or credits). Next, a discussion concerning the rationale for deductions as part of the tax code is provided. Because some deductions are classified as tax expenditures, or losses in federal revenue, they might be of interest to Congress from a budgetary perspective. The final section of this report includes tables that summarize each individual tax deduction, under current law. Many of these deductions are part of the permanent income tax code. The American Taxpayer and Relief Act of 2012 (P.L. 112- 240) extended several temporary provisions through 2012 and 2013.

INTRODUCTION

This report provides an overview of income tax deductions for individuals. A tax deduction reduces the amount of a tax filer's income that is subject to taxation, ultimately reducing the tax filer's tax liability. Every tax filer has the option to claim deductions when filing their income tax return. However, some tax filers and policymakers may not have detailed knowledge of tax deductions, including future changes in the requirements to claim certain deductions. In addition, tax deductions may be of interest to Congress from a budgetary perspective, as some deductions are classified as *tax expenditures*, and result in losses in federal revenue.

This report first describes what tax deductions are, how they vary in their effects on reducing taxable income, and how they differ from other provisions (e.g., exclusions or credits). Next, it discusses the rationale for deductions as part of the tax code. The final section includes tables that summarize each individual tax deduction, under current law.

This report focuses on the standard treatment of tax deductions for individuals under the individual income tax code. As such, the following are beyond the scope of this report:

- the different treatment of deductions under the alternative minimum tax for individuals,[1]
- tax deductions for businesses under the individual income tax code,[2] and
- options for reforming itemized deductions.[3]

CALCULATING THE INDIVIDUAL INCOME TAX

To understand what tax deductions are, it is helpful to first understand how a tax filer calculates individual income tax liability. **Figure 1** provides an overview of how a tax filer calculates his or her federal *tax liability*.[4] To calculate taxes owed (tax liability), tax filers first add up all of their forms of income (see step 1 in **Figure 1**) to calculate their gross income. Next, the tax filer subtracts any *above-the-line* deductions to calculate their *adjusted gross income*, or AGI (step 2). AGI is often referred to as "the line." Then, the tax filer subtracts *personal exemptions*, or fixed dollar amounts per spouse and dependent child (step 3). The tax filer then subtracts the greater of either the sum of all of their *below-the-line*, or *itemized deductions*, or the *standard deduction*, which is a fixed amount based on filing status, in order to arrive at taxable income (step 4). The marginal tax rates are applied to taxable income (step 5) to arrive at a preliminary tax liability.

Finally, tax credits are subtracted from preliminary tax liability (step 6) to arrive at final tax liability.

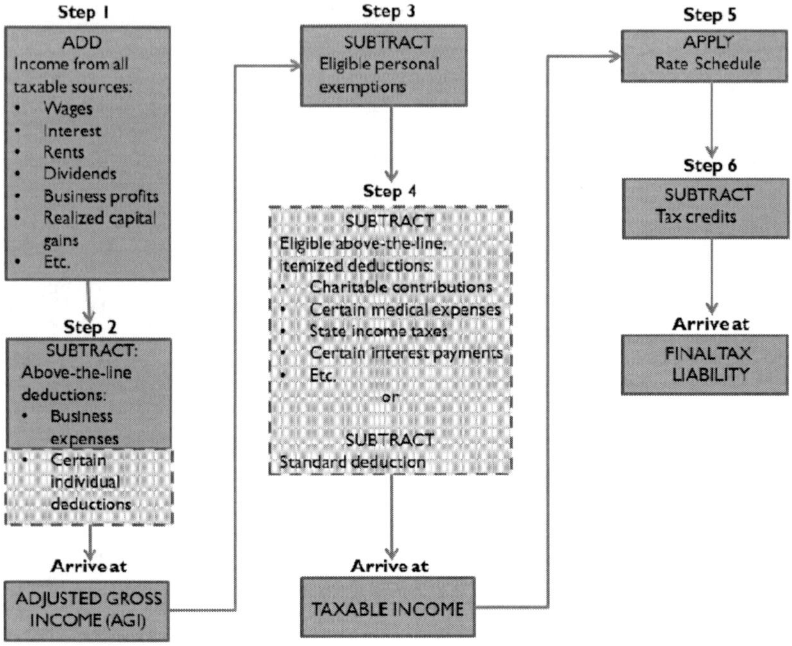

Source: Harvey S. Rosen, *Public Finance*, 7th ed. (New York, NY: McGraw-Hill Irwin, 2005), p. 360.

Figure 1. Computation of Federal Personal Income Tax Liability.

WHAT ARE TAX DEDUCTIONS?

Simply stated, deductions reduce taxable income. Each deduction reduces tax liability by the amount of deduction times the tax filer's marginal tax rate. In contrast, a tax credit reduces tax liability on a dollar-for-dollar basis because it would be applied *after* the marginal tax rate schedule. An individual in a 35% tax bracket would receive a reduction in taxes of $35 for each $100 deduction while an individual in a 25% tax bracket would receive a reduction in taxes of $25 for each $100 deduction. Hence, the same deduction can be worth different amounts to different tax filers depending on their marginal tax bracket. The tax savings from deductions are generally equal to the tax filer's marginal tax rate times the amount of the deduction. So higher-income tax filers typically benefit more than lower-income tax filers from deductions.

Deductions serve four main purposes in the tax code.[5] First, they can account for large, unusual, and necessary personal expenditures, such as the deduction for extraordinary medical expenses. Second, they are used to encourage certain types of activities, such as homeownership and charitable contributions. Third, they account for and ease the burden the burden of paying for non-federal forms of taxes, such as state and local taxes. Fourth, deductions adjust for the expenses of earning income, such as deductions for work-related employee expenses.

The following sections define each form of deduction and explain in greater detail how deductions are used in the calculation of an individual's tax liability.

ABOVE-VS.-BELOW-THE-LINE DEDUCTIONS

To arrive at final tax liability, all taxpayers may be able to claim above-the-line deductions whether they claim itemized deductions or the standard deduction. Each of these deductions has a specific line on the Form 1040 (e.g., line 34 for the deduction of student loan interest). Figure 2 shows how tax deductions appear on the IRS Form 1040.

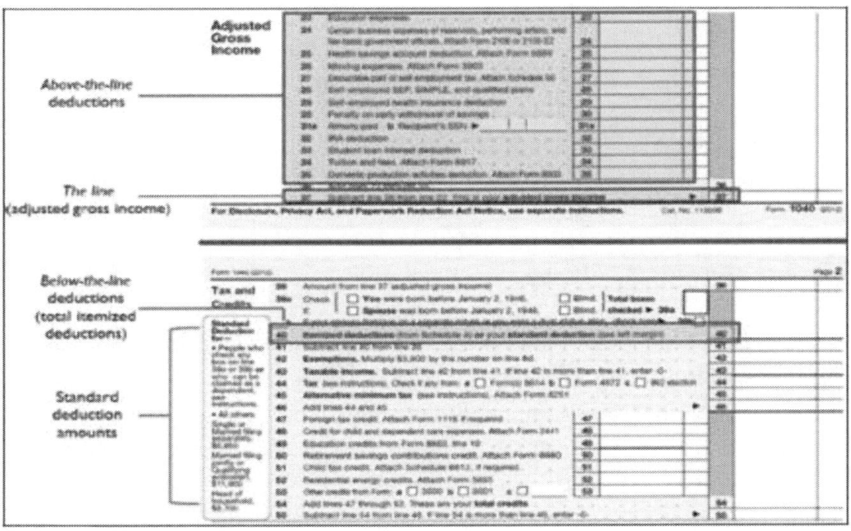

Source: Internal Revenue Service, 2012Form 1040, at http://www.irs.gov /file_source/pub/irs-pdf/f1040.pdf.

Figure 2. Above- Versus Below-the-Line Deductions on the IRS Form 1040.

These deductions are commonly referred to as *above-the-line* deductions, because they reduce a tax filer's AGI (the line). Above-the-line deductions are sometimes also called *adjustments* to income, because they generally represent costs incurred to earn income. In contrast, itemized and standard deductions are sometimes referred to *below-the-line* deductions, because they are applied *after* AGI is calculated to arrive at taxable income.

Above-the-line deductions may provide additional benefits to some tax filers seeking to claim certain tax preferences. A number of tax provisions have a phaseout of benefits as income increases. The higher the AGI, the less likely the tax filer will be able to claim a larger value of the tax preference. Tax deductions that lower AGI increase the likelihood that the tax filer will be able to claim a larger value of the tax preference.

ITEMIZED VERSUS STANDARD DEDUCTIONS

As previously discussed, tax filers have the option to claim either a standard deduction or the sum of their itemized deductions. Whichever deduction the tax filer claims—standard or itemized— the deduction amount is subtracted from AGI to arrive at final tax liability.

Standard Deduction

The *standard deduction* is a fixed amount, based on filing status, available to all taxpayers. In contrast to those itemizing their deductions, tax filers do not have to provide additional documentation in order to claim the standard deduction.

The standard deduction was introduced into the federal tax code with the passage of the Individual Income Tax Act of 1944 (P.L. 78-315) primarily to simplify tax administration and compliance. At the time of passage, it was noted that taxpayers generally had little idea about what deductions were allowable and few taxpayers kept accurate records. Thus, the enactment of the standard deduction reduced excessive unsupportable claims of deductions, although at the same time it permitted many taxpayers to take a deduction in excess of what they would have been allowed if they had been required to itemized their deductions.

Today it is also viewed as performing a social welfare purpose. The social welfare purpose of the standard deduction was introduced with the minimum standard deduction in the Revenue Act of 1964 (P.L. 88-272). Under this minimum standard deduction provision, a taxpayer was assured a minimum amount of deductions from his or her income. The personal exemptions combined with the standard deduction amount are designed to remove low-income households from the tax rolls.

The calculation of the standard deduction has changed over time. In 1944, it was equal to 10% of AGI, up to a maximum of $1,000. In 1964, a minimum standard deduction was introduced as a fixed value of $200 plus $100 for each exemption with a ceiling of $1,000 if married filing jointly.[6] The value of the standard deduction, including both the percent of AGI and the maximum value, was increased multiple times from 1969 to 1975. The minimum standard deduction and the deduction were merged in 1977 into a flat standard deduction of $2,200 (single) and $3,200 (married filing jointly).[7] The Economic Recovery Tax Act of 1981 (P.L. 97-34) indexed standard deduction amounts for inflation, beginning in 1985.[8] The standard deduction has been increased over time, such as with the Tax Reform Act of 1986 (TRA86; P.L. 99-514).

The Economic Growth and Tax Relief Reconciliation Act of 2001 (EGTRRA; P.L. 107-16) phased out part of the so-called marriage penalty associated with the federal tax code, where the standard deduction for joint filers was less than twice the single filer amount. EGTRRA increased the deduction for joint filers to 200% of singles. This provision, most recently extended by Tax Relief, Unemployment Insurance Reauthorization and Job Creation Act of 2010 (P.L. 111-312), will expire in 2012. Under current law, the standard deduction for married couples filing jointly will be equal to 167% of upper limit for singles for the 2013 tax year and beyond.[9]

The standard deduction amount varies depending on the filing status of the tax unit (i.e., single, married filing jointly, married filing separately, or head of household), whether the tax filer is over the age of 65, and whether the tax filer is blind. For the 2012 tax year the inflation-adjusted standard deductions are as follows:

- $11,900 for married filing jointly or qualified widow(er)s;
- $5,950 for single tax filers and married filing separately; and
- $8,700 for tax filers who qualify as the head of a household.[10]

In addition, there is a standard deduction available for an individual who can be claimed as a dependent on another person's tax return. The standard deduction for a dependent is generally limited to the greater of $950 (in 2012) or the individual's earned income for the year, plus $300 (but not more than the regular standard deduction amount of $5,950 for single tax filers).

The additional standard deductions for those aged 65 or older and those who are legally blind are increased by $1,450 if single or head of household and $1,150 if married filing jointly. These increases apply per classification and are added above the base standard deduction amounts listed above. Thus, a 70-year-old blind and single tax filer would be eligible for a $2,900 increase ($1,450 for being 65 or older, and $1,450 for being blind) in his or her standard deduction. These amounts are adjusted annually for inflation.[11]

Itemized Deductions

Alternatively, tax filers claiming *itemized deductions* must list each item separately on their tax return and be able to provide documentation (i.e., in the event of an IRS audit) that the expenditures have been made.

Tax filers have been able to itemize their deductions since the Revenue Act of 1913 (P.L. 63-16), which created the first permanent federal income tax. Deductions for interest paid or unexpected casualty losses were early provisions in the federal income tax code because many businesses were sole proprietorships (i.e., pass-through entities) where the owner was personally liable for the costs of doing business. Itemized deductions have been reduced or limited in eligibility, most notably with TRA86. For example, TRA86 eliminated deductions for consumer interest and enacted more complex rules for deducting investment interest.[12]

Only individuals with aggregate itemized deductions greater than the standard deduction find it worthwhile to itemize. Itemized deductions are claimed on the IRS Schedule A form.[13] Itemized deductions are allowed for a variety of purposes. A detailed summary of the requirements and limits for each of these provisions, and other itemized deductions, is included in **Table 2**, at the end of this report.

Some itemized deductions can only be claimed if they meet or exceed minimum threshold amounts (usually a certain percentage of AGI) in order to simplify tax administration and compliance. For example, a tax filer must meet a certain threshold (or a *floor*) to deduct a casualty, disaster, or theft loss.

Certain itemized deductions are treated as miscellaneous itemized deductions, which are allowed only to the extent that their total *exceeds* 2% of the individual tax filer's AGI. This floor makes it simpler for a tax filer to choose whether he or she would be better off itemizing the deductions or choosing to claim the standard deduction, and it helps to ensure that the IRS is only reviewing documentation of fewer, larger events rather than many, smaller events. Any restriction placed upon an itemized deduction generally applies *prior* to the 2% AGI floor.[14] An example of an expense subject to the combined 2% of AGI floor for miscellaneous deductions is the 50% reduction for unreimbursed meals while traveling away from home on business.

In addition, some deductions are subject to a cap (also known as a *ceiling*) in benefits or eligibility. Caps are meant to reduce the extent that tax provisions can distort economic behavior, limit revenue losses, or reduce the availability of the deduction to higher-income tax filers. For example, the home mortgage interest itemized deduction is limited to mortgage debt in the amount of up to $1 million for married couples filing jointly ($500,000 for individuals or married filing separate).[15] This ceiling is intended to limit incentives for higher-income tax filers to finance their home purchases with deductible interest.

Pease Limit on Itemized Deductions for Higher-Income Tax Filers

There is a limitation on the *value* of itemized deductions that certain, higher-income tax filers can claim. The limitation on itemized deductions was initially included in the Omnibus Budget Reconciliation Act of 1990 (P.L. 101-508), drafted by Representative Donald Pease of Ohio. Commonly referred to as "Pease" by tax analysts, it effectively increases taxes on high-income tax filers without explicitly increasing tax rates.

Pease's limitations are triggered by an AGI threshold.[16] The number or total amount of itemized deductions claimed by a tax filer does *not* determine whether he or she is subject to Pease. Pease affects tax filers above the inflation-adjusted AGI thresholds who itemize deductions. For these tax filers, the total of certain itemized deductions is reduced by 3% of the amount of AGI exceeding the threshold.[17] The total reduction, however, cannot be greater than 80% of the deductions (and the tax filer always has the option of taking the standard deduction). Consequently, the effective marginal tax rate for these tax filers will be 3% higher than their statutory marginal tax rate.[18]

Pease was in effect from 1991 to 2009, and was fully repealed from 2010 to 2012.[19] The Economic Growth and Tax Relief Reconciliation Act of 2001 (P.L. 107-16) included the phased-in repeal of Pease between 2006 and 2009. Pease was scheduled to be reinstituted beginning with the 2011 tax year, but the reintroduction was postponed until the 2013 tax year by the Tax Relief, Unemployment Insurance Reauthorization, and Job Creation Act of 2010 (P.L. 111-312).

The American Taxpayer and Relief Act of 2012 (ATRA; P.L. 112-240) restored Pease for tax years 2013 and beyond. Prior to the enactment of ATRA, Pease's income thresholds would have been triggered at $177,550 for single filers for 2013.[20] After the enactment of ATRA, Pease applies to tax filers with an AGI of:

- $250,000, if single;
- $275,000, if head of household;
- $300,000, if married filing jointly or a surviving spouse; or
- $150,000, if married, filing separately.[21]

SUMMARY OF INDIVIDUAL TAX DEDUCTIONS

Table 1 and **Table 2** provide a summary of above- and belowthe-line tax deductions, respectively.[22] The first column provides a reference to where the provision can be found on the Form 1040 (if an above-the-line deduction) or on the Schedule A form (if a below-the-line, itemized tax deduction). The provision column contains a reference to where the provision can be found in the Internal Revenue Code (IRC), which is Title 26 of the U.S. Code. A brief summary of the provision follows in the adjacent column. When applicable, annual limits (whether they are floors or ceilings) and income limits and phaseouts are provided.[23] The last column provides the tax expenditure amount for FY2013 and FY2014.[24]

Abbreviations Used in Table 1 and Table 2

S: Single tax filer
MFJ: Married, filing jointly
MFS: Married, filing separately
HOH: Head of household filer
SS: Surviving spouse filer

Table 1. Summary of Above-the-Line, Tax Deductions for Individuals

1040 Line[a]	Provision	Summary of Deductible Expense	Annual Deduction Limit $250 None	Income Limits and Phaseouts	Tax Expenditure, in Billions[b]
23	Educator expenses IRC §62	An eligible employee of a public (including charter) and private elementary or secondary school may deduct ordinary and necessary expenses paid in connection with books, supplies, equipment (including computers and software), and other materials used in the classroom. The American Taxpayer Relief Act of 2012 (ATRA; P.L. 112-240) extended this provision for 2013.		None	FY2013: $0.2 FY2014: $0.1
24	Certain reimbursed business expenses of reservists, performing artists, and fee-basis government officials IRC §162(p), 62(a)(2)(E), and 62(a)(1)	Certain reimbursed business expenses of National Guard and Reserve members who traveled more than 100 miles from home to perform their services; performing arts-related expenses; and business expenses of fee-basis state or local government officials.		None	FY2013: $0.1 FY2014: $0.1
25	Health savings account (HSA) contributions IRC §223	Eligible individuals can establish Health Savings Accounts (HSAs) and fund these accounts when they have qualifying high deductible health insurance	2012: $3,100 for individual plans and $6,250 for family plans; individuals aged 55 or older can contribute an additional $1,000. 2013:	None	FY2013: $1.8 FY2014: $2.1

Table 1. (Continued)

1040 Line[a]	Provision	Summary of Deductible Expense	Annual Deduction Limit $250 None	Income Limits and Phaseouts	Tax Expenditure, in Billions[b]
		(insurance with a deductible of at least $1,200 for single coverage and $2,400 for family coverage, plus other criteria described below) and no other health care coverage, with some exceptions.	$3,250 for individual plans and $6,450 for family plans; individuals aged 55 or older can contribute an additional $1,000.		
25	Archer medical savings account (MSA) contributions IRC §223	Contributions toward Archer medical savings account (MSAs). Archer MSAs are tax-exempt trust or custodial accounts, established with a U.S. financial institution, used to save money exclusively for future medical expenses. Individuals must meet the following requirements to be eligible for an Archer MSA, including: having a high deductible health plan (HDHP); having no other health or Medicare coverage; and being either a small employer or self-employed (or the spouse of a self-employed individual).	(1) Cannot exceed a taxpayer's net earned income from the business in which the health insurance plan was established. (2) For those with individual coverage: 65% of the annual deductible. For those with family coverage: 75% of the annual deductible.	None	[dm]

1040 Line[a]	Provision	Summary of Deductible Expense	Annual Deduction Limit $250 None	Income Limits and Phaseouts	Tax Expenditure, in Billions[b]
26	Work-related moving expenses IRC §217	Unreimbursed moving expenses incurred during the taxable year in connection with the commencement of work by the taxpayer as an employee or as a self-employed individual at a new principal place of work that is at least 50 miles farther from the prior residence.	None	None	NA
28	Retirement plan contributions for the self-employed IRC §401-408	A self-employed individual may deduct contributions to a Simplified Employment Plan (SEP), Savings Incentive Match Plan for Employees of Small Employers (SIMPLE), or Keogh plan.	Contributions cannot exceed an amount equal to 25% of pay up to a maximum amount indexed to inflation: SEP and Keogh: $50,000 (2012), $51,000 (2013). SIMPLE: $11,500 (2012), and $12,000 (2013). Participants aged 50 and older can make additional contributions of up to $2,500 in both 2012 and 2013.	None	NA
29	Health insurance premiums for the self-employed IRC §162(I)	A self-employed individual may deduct the premium costs of health insurance or long-term care insurance as long as he or she is not eligible to participate in a plan, in a given month, sponsored by his or her employer or the spouse's employer.	(1) Cannot exceed a taxpayer's net earned income from the business in which the health insurance plan was established, less the deductions for 50% of the self-employment tax and any contributions to	None	FY2013: $5.2 FY2014: $5.6

Table 1. (Continued)

1040 Line[a]	Provision	Summary of Deductible Expense	Annual Deduction Limit $250 None	Income Limits and Phaseouts	Tax Expenditure, in Billions[b]
			qualified pension plans. (2) If a self-employed individual claims an itemized deduction for medical expenses, those expenses must be reduced by any deduction for health insurance premiums.		
31	Alimony paid IRC §215	Alimony and separate maintenance payments are income to the recipient and are deductible by the payor if certain requirements are met [USC §62(a)(10), 71, and 215]. Child support is not tax deductible.	None	None	NA
32	Retirement savings, including traditional individual retirement accounts (IRAs) IRC §219	Taxpayers may deduct qualified retirement contributions, such as a 401(k) plan or a traditional IRA, generally limited to $5,000 (increased by $1,000 of catch-up contributions for taxpayers aged 50 and over), adjusted for inflation occurring after 2008 (it remains $5,000 for 2012).	The lesser of $5,000 or 100% of compensation. The ceiling is indexed for inflation in $500 increments. Individuals aged 50 and older may make an additional catch-up contribution of $1,000. A married taxpayer may make deductible contributions to an IRA for the benefit of the	For active participants in certain pension plans, the deduction amount is phased-out proportionately over the following inflation-adjusted AGI ranges: MFJ: $92,000-$112,000 (2012), $95,000-$115,000	FY2013: $14.9 FY2013: $17.6

1040 Line[a]	Provision	Summary of Deductible Expense	Annual Deduction Limit $250 None	Income Limits and Phaseouts	Tax Expenditure, in Billions[b]
		ATRA permanently expanded the availability of "in-plan Roth conversions," allowing virtually all traditional employer-sponsored retirement account balances [like funds in a 401(k) plan] to be transferred to employer-sponsored Roth accounts [like Roth 401(k) plans]. By electing to convert a non-Roth account to a Roth account, an employee pays tax at the time the funds are rolled over or converted. However, when an employee ultimately withdraws funds from these Roth accounts they will not be subject to taxation.[c]	spouse up to: 2012: $5,000 2013: $5,500	(2013). Taxpayers whose spouses are active participants: $173,000-$183,000 (2012), $178,000-$188,000 (2013). Other taxpayers: $58,000-$68,000 (2012), $59,000-$69,000 (2013).	
33	Interest on Education Loans IRC §221	Interest paid on a qualified student loan is deductible in the year that the interest was paid.	$2,500, subject to income phaseouts: 2012: MFJ: $100,000-$130,000. Other taxpayers: $50,000-$60,000. 2013: MFJ: $60,000-$75,000. Other taxpayers: $40,000-$55,000.	Inflation adjusted phaseout: MFJ: $125,000-$155,000 (2012), $75,000-$90,000 (2013). Other taxpayers: $60,000-$75,000 (2012), $50,000-$65,000 (2013).	FY2013: $1.3 FY2013: $1.4

Table 1. (Continued)

1040 Line[a]	Provision	Summary of Deductible Expense	Annual Deduction Limit $250 None	Income Limits and Phaseouts	Tax Expenditure, in Billions[b]
34	Qualified Tuition and Related Expenses IRC §222	Includes costs related to qualified tuition, fees, room and board, books, and supplies. The ATRA (P.L. 112-240) extended this provision for 2013.	Up to $4,000 or $2,000, depending on AGI.	Taxpayers could deduct up to $4,000 or up to $2,000 of qualified tuition and related expenses depending on their AGI fell between the following ranges in 2011: $65,000 or less ($130,000 MFJ): $4,000. $65,001- $80,000 ($160,000 MFJ): $2,000.	FY2013: $0.7 FY2013: $0.2

Source: Internal Revenue Service (IRS), *Tax Guide 2012 for Individuals*, Publication 17, at http://www.irs.gov/pub/irs-pdf/p17.pdf; IRS, various publications, at http://www.irs.gov/pub/; IRS, 2012Form 1040, at http://www.irs.gov/pub/irs-pdf/f1040.pdf; IRS, Cost-of-Living (COLA) Increases for Dollar Limitations on Benefits and Contributions, at http://www.irs.gov/Retirement-Plans/COLA-Increases-for-Dollar-Limitations-on-Benefits-and-Contributions; Joint Committee on Taxation, Estimates of Federal Tax Expenditures, For Fiscal Years 2012-2017, 113th Congress, 1st session, February 1, 2013, JCS-1-13 (Washington: GPO, 2013); and U.S. Congress, Senate Committee on the Budget, *Tax Expenditures: Compendium of Background Materials on Individual Provisions*, committee print, prepared by the Congressional Research Service, 111th Congress, 2nd session, December 2010, 111-58 (Washington: GPO, 2010).

Notes:

a. Line numbers refer to the 2012 Schedule A to the Form 1040.

b. Tax expenditures estimates are for individuals only, not corporations. Estimates below JCT's *de-minimus* amount of $50 million, as per its February 2013 estimates, are denoted by [dm]. Provisions without a JCT tax expenditure amount are denoted by NA.

c. For more information on ATRA's changes to the tax treatment of IRAs, see CRS Report R42894, *An Overview of the Tax Provisions in the American Taxpayer Relief Act of 2012* , by Margot L. Crandall-Hollick.

Table 2. Summary of Below-the-Line, Itemized Tax Deductions for Individuals

Schedule A Line[a]	Provision	Summary of Deductible Expense	Annual Deduction Floor or Limit	Income Limits and Phaseouts, 2012	Tax Expenditure, in Billions[b]
1	Medical and dental expenses IRC §213	Includes the diagnosis, cure, mitigation, treatment, or prevention of disease, or for the purpose of affecting any structure or function of the body; lodging and transportation costs related to essential medical care; qualified long-term care services; insurance covering medical care for any qualified long-term care insurance contract; and prescribed drugs.	2012: Expenses are deductible only if they exceed the floor of 7.5% of adjusted gross income (AGI). 2013: This floor is increased to 10% of AGI.	None	FY2013: $11.4 FY2013: $12.4
5 and 7	State and local nonbusiness, income, sales, and personal property taxes IRC §164	Taxpayers who itemize can choose between deducting either state and local income taxes or sales taxes, but not both. State and local income taxes are withheld from wages during the year, as they appear on Form W-2. Non-business state or local property taxes are also deductible. The American Taxpayer Relief Act of 2012 (P.L. 112-240) extended the option to deduct sales taxes in lieu of income taxes for 2013.	None	None	FY2013: $50.3 FY2014: $51.8

Table 2. (Continued)

Schedule A Line[a]	Provision	Summary of Deductible Expense	Annual Deduction Floor or Limit	Income Limits and Phaseouts, 2012	Tax Expenditure, in Billions[b]
6	Real estate taxes IRC §164	Tax filers can claim an itemized deduction for property taxes paid on owner-occupied residences.	None	None	FY2013: $27.0 FY2014: $28.6
8	Federal estate tax on income in respect of a decedent (IRD) IRC §691(c)	The IRS allows any recipient of current or future IRD to deduct any properly allocable expenses against the income that was not claimed on the decedent's final tax return for estate tax purposes. Common items include fiduciary fees, commissions paid to dispose of assets, and state income taxes.	None	None	NA
10-11	Home mortgage interest and other provisions related to homeownership IRC §163(h)	Interest paid on an eligible mortgage secured by a principal or secondary residence is deductible. Interest can also be deducted on home equity loans. The sum of the acquisition indebtedness and home equity debt cannot exceed the fair market value of the home(s). Home equity debt means any loan whose purpose is not to acquire, to construct, or substantially to improve a qualified home, or any loan whose purpose was to substantially improve a qualified home but exceeds the home acquisition debt limit.	Mortgage interest paid on primary and secondary residences are deductible up to: MFJ: the first $1,000,000 of a mortgage. Other taxpayers: the first $500,000 of a mortgage. The deduction for interest on home equity debt is limited to interest associated with the first $100,000 in home equity debt combined from a primary and secondary residence.	None	FY2013: $69.7 FY2013: $71.7

Schedule A Line[a]	Provision	Summary of Deductible Expense	Annual Deduction Floor or Limit	Income Limits and Phaseouts, 2012	Tax Expenditure, in Billions[b]
13	Home mortgage insurance premiums IRC §163	Qualified mortgage insurance premiums are deductible if the insurance policy covers home acquisition debt on a primary or secondary residence. Qualified mortgage insurance means mortgage insurance obtained from the Department of Veterans Affairs (VA), the Federal Housing Authority (FHA), the Rural Housing Administration (RHA), and private mortgage insurance as defined by the Homeowners Protection Act of 1988. The ATRA (P.L. 112-240) extended this provision for 2013.	None	Deduction is reduced by 10% for each $1,000 a filer's income is over the following AGI thresholds: MFJ: $100,000 (2012). Other taxpayers: $50,000 (2012). And completely phases out by: MFJ: $109,000 (2012). Other taxpayers: $54,500 (2012).	[dm]
14	Investment interest IRC §163	Tax filers can deduct investment interest, or money borrowed to purchase taxable interests. Leftover investment interest expenses can be carried over for use in future years, without expiration.	Interest expenses are deductible up to the amount of any net investment income.	None	NA

Table 2. (Continued)

Schedule A Line[a]	Provision	Summary of Deductible Expense	Annual Deduction Floor or Limit	Income Limits and Phaseouts, 2012	Tax Expenditure, in Billions[b]
16-18	Charitable contributions IRC §170 and 642(c)	Subject to certain limitations, charitable contributions may be deducted by individuals, corporations, and estates and trusts. The contributions must be made to specific types of organizations, including scientific, literary, or educational organizations [as specified by IRC §501(c)(3)].	Can deduct contributions up to 50% of AGI that go to 501(c)(3) organizations. For contributions to non-operating foundations and organizations, deductibility is limited to the lesser of 30% of the taxpayer's contribution base, or the excess of 50% of the contribution base for the tax year over the amount of contributions which qualified for the 50% deduction ceiling (including carryovers from previous years). Gifts of capital gain property to these organizations are limited to 20% of AGI.	None	FY2013: $39.0c FY2014: $43.6
20	Casualty, disaster, or theft losses IRC §165(c)(3), 165(e), 165(h) -165(k).	Applies to non-business property lost due to fire, storm, shipwreck, or other casualty, or from theft. The cause of the loss should be considered a sudden, unexpected, and unusual event. The loss must be sustained (e.g., without expectation of being compensated).	Limited to losses in excess of $500 per event and 10% of AGI combined.	None	FY2013: $0.3 FY2014: $0.3

Schedule A Line[a]	Provision	Summary of Deductible Expense	Annual Deduction Floor or Limit	Income Limits and Phaseouts, 2012	Tax Expenditure, in Billions[b]
21	Unreimbursed employee expenses IRC §162	Includes miscellaneous job-related unreimbursed expenses, such as travel costs, union dues, job-related education, uniforms, and subscriptions to professional journals.	Subject to the combined expenses floor in excess of 2% of AGI.	None	NA
22	Tax preparation fees IRC §212	Tax preparation fees and expenses, including the cost of tax preparation software programs and tax publications, are deductible.	Subject to the combined expenses floor in excess of 2% of AGI.	None	NA
23	Other financial and investment expenses IRC §212	Includes expenses such as investment management fees, safe deposit box rental fees, and transportation to an investment broker's or advisor's office.	Subject to the combined expenses floor in excess of 2% of AGI.	None	NAd
28	Gambling losses that offset gambling winnings IRC §165	Wagering losses are deductible only to the extent of the taxpayer's gains from similar transactions (USC §165(d); Reg Sec 1.165-10). Nonbusiness gambling losses are deductible only as itemized deductions. If gambling is conducted as a business, the losses are deductible as business losses, but only to the extent of gains.	Subject to the combined expenses floor in excess of 2% of AGI. Gambling losses claimed as a deduction cannot exceed winnings in the same year.	None	NA

Table 2. (Continued)

Schedule A Line[a]	Provision	Summary of Deductible Expense	Annual Deduction Floor or Limit	Income Limits and Phaseouts, 2012	Tax Expenditure, in Billions[b]
28	Impairment-related work expenses of a person with disabilities ICR §67(d)	Qualified impairment-related work expenses are deductible. These include expenses, such as: prosthetics, specialized office equipment, supplies, or an attendant during work hours.	None	None	NA

Source: Internal Revenue Service (IRS), *Tax Guide 2012 for Individuals*, Publication 17, at http://www.irs.gov/pub/irs-pdf/p17.pdf; IRS, various publications, at http://www.irs.gov/pub/; IRS, 2012 Schedule A (Form 1040), at http://www.irs.gov/pub/irs-pdf/f1040sa.pdf; Joint Committee on Taxation, Estimates of Federal Tax Expenditures, For Fiscal Years 2012-2017, 113th Congress, 1st session, February 1, 2013, JCS-1-13 (Washington: GPO, 2013); and U.S. Congress, Senate Committee on the Budget, *Tax Expenditures: Compendium of Background Materials on Individual Provisions*, committee print, prepared by the Congressional Research Service, 111th Congress, 2nd session, December 2010, 111-58 (Washington: GPO, 2010).

Notes:

a. Line numbers refer to the 2012 Schedule A to the Form 1040.

b. Tax expenditures estimates are for individuals only, not corporations. Estimates below JCT's *de-minimus* amount of $50 million, as per its February 2013 estimates, are denoted by [dm]. Provisions without a JCT tax expenditure amount are denoted by NA.

c. This estimate is the sum of the three different categories of charitable giving included in JCT's tax expenditures estimates that were conducted in 2013.

d. JCT did not provide a tax expenditure estimate for this provision, as it is considered to be a negative tax expenditure (i.e., revenue net-gain).

Tax expenditures are defined under the Congressional Budget and Impoundment Control Act of 1974 (P.L. 93-344) as "revenue losses attributable to provisions of the Federal tax laws which allow a special exclusion, exemption, or deduction from gross income or which provide a special credit, a preferential rate of tax, or a deferral of tax liability."[25] Tax expenditure estimates are based on current law, which does not assume extensions of temporary provisions that are subject to expire within the time period observed. Not all tax deductions have JCT tax expenditure estimates, as some provisions are estimated to result in revenue losses less than $50 million per fiscal year (JCT's *de minimus* level). In addition, some tax deductions are not considered tax expenditures for various, other reasons.[26] For example, the deduction for uncompensated employee expenses is considered an appropriate measure to adjust a tax filer's AGI.

End Notes

[1] See CRS Report RL30149, *The Alternative Minimum Tax for Individuals*, by Steven Maguire.

[2] Some of the deductions reported on the Internal Revenue Service Form 1040 relate to business expenses, as some business are organized as pass-through entities. Pass-through entities get their name from the fact that the business's income passes-through to the owner, as opposed to being claimed separately by the business. However, the tax treatment of business income through the individual tax code is beyond the scope of this report. For more information on pass-through entities, see CRS Report R40748, *Business Organizational Choices: Taxation and Responses to Legislative Changes*, by Mark P. Keightley.

[3] For example, see CRS Report R42435, *The Challenge of Individual Income Tax Reform: An Economic Analysis of Tax Base Broadening*, by Jane G. Gravelle and Thomas L. Hungerford; and CRS Report RL33755, *Federal Income Tax Treatment of the Family*, by Jane G. Gravelle.

[4] For a more detailed description of each of these tax terms, see CRS Report RL30110, *Federal Individual Income Tax Terms: An Explanation*, by Mark P. Keightley. For a general explanation of the federal tax system, see CRS Report RL32808, *Overview of the Federal Tax System*, by Molly F. Sherlock and Donald J. Marples.

[5] Joseph A. Pechman, *Federal Tax Policy*, 3rd ed. (Washington, DC: Brookings Institution Press, 1977), pp. 85-88.

[6] CRS Report 80-31, *Historical Summary of Selected Features of the Individual Income Tax*, by George J. Leibowitz and Jane G. Gravelle. This archived report, last updated by Cheryl Savage Newton in 1980, is available upon request.

[7] Ibid.

[8] Jon Bakija and Eugene Steuerle, "Individual Income Taxation Since 1948," *National Tax Journal*, vol. 44, no. 4 (December 1991), p. 453.

[9] See CRS Report R42485, *An Overview of Tax Provisions Expiring in 2012*, by Margot L. Crandall-Hollick.

[10] See Internal Revenue Service, *In 2012, Many Tax Benefits Increase Due to Inflation Adjustments*, press release, October 20, 2011, at http://www.irs.gov/uac/In-2012,-Many-Tax-Benefits-Increase-Due-to-Inflation-Adjustments.

[11] For 2013, these standard deductions are as follows: $12,200 married filing jointly, $6,100 single, and $8,950 for head of household. See U.S. Congress, Joint Committee on Taxation, *Overview of the Federal Tax System As in Effect for 2013*, committee print, 113th Cong., 1st sess., January 8, 2013, JCX-2-13R (Washington: GPO, 2013), p. 4.

[12] See Sally Wallace, "Itemized Deductions," in *Encyclopedia of Taxation and Tax Policy*, ed. Joseph J. Cordes, Robert D. Ebel, and Jane G. Gravelle (Washington, DC: Urban Institute Press, 2000), p. 215. For an explanation of reforms to particular itemized tax deductions in the Tax Reform Act of 1986, see U.S. Congress, Joint Committee on Taxation, *General Explanation of the Tax Reform Act of 1986*, committee print, 100th Cong., 1st sess., May 4, 1687, JCS-10-87 (Washington: GPO, 1987).

[13] Internal Revenue Service, 2012 Schedule A (Form 1040), at http://www.irs.gov/pub/irs-pdf/f1040sa.pdf.

[14] Internal Revenue Code (IRC) Section 162(a).

[15] IRC §163(h).

[16] Ibid.

[17] The deductions not subject to the Pease limitation are medical and dental expenses, investment interest, qualified charitable contributions, and casualty and theft losses.

[18] The statutory tax rate is the marginal tax rate a tax filer faces based on their AGI. In contrast, the effective marginal tax rate is the net rate a taxpayer pays on an increment of income that includes all forms of taxes, including the different rate for itemized deductions under Pease. The average effective tax rate is calculated by dividing total tax liability by total gross income.

[19] For more information on the Pease limitation and sample calculations, see CRS Report R41796, *Deficit Reduction: The Economic and Tax Revenue Effects of the Personal Exemption Phaseout (PEP) and the Limitation on Itemized Deductions (Pease)*, by Thomas L. Hungerford.

[20] U.S. Congress, Joint Committee on Taxation, *Description of Revenue Provisions Contained in the President's Fiscal Year 2013 Budget Proposal*, committee print, 112th Cong., 2nd sess., June 2012, JCS-2-12 (Washington: GPO, 2012), p. 200.

[21] These Pease income thresholds will be adjusted for inflation for tax years after 2013.

[22] For more information about each provision, please refer to the latest IRS tax guide or the specific Internal Revenue Code provision within the U.S. Code. These summary tables are not meant to be a substitute for professional tax assistance.

[23] Some provisions in the tax code are phased out (i.e., their value is reduced as income rises) for higher-income taxpayers as a way to target tax benefits on middle- and lower-income households and to limit the loss of revenue.

[24] Joint Committee on Taxation, Estimates of Federal Tax Expenditures, For Fiscal Years 2012-2017, 113th Congress, 1st session, February 1, 2013, JCS-1-13 (Washington: GPO, 2013).

[25] P.L. 93-344, Section 3(3).

[26] For a discussion of the debate over what is and what is not a *tax expenditure*, see Leonard E. Burman, "Is the Tax Expenditure Concept Still Relevant?," *National Tax Journal*, vol. 56, no. 3 (September 2003), pp. 613-627, and Donald B. Marron, "Spending in Disguise," *National Affairs*, no. 8 (Summer 2011), at http://www.nationalaffairs.com/publications/detail/spending-in-disguise.

INDEX

A

adjustment, 46
age, 45, 83
Alaska, 54
assessment, 39
assets, 11, 13, 21, 36, 37, 45, 46, 53, 76, 94
audit, 45, 63, 84
automobiles, 21
awareness, 39

B

base, vii, viii, 1, 2, 3, 9, 10, 18, 22, 27, 29, 30, 32, 35, 40, 44, 47, 57, 84, 96
basic needs, 57
behavioral change, 72
behaviors, 8, 73
benefits, vii, x, xi, 1, 4, 9, 12, 17, 19, 21, 22, 23, 28, 29, 30, 35, 36, 37, 38, 39, 40, 41, 42, 43, 44, 45, 46, 57, 58, 62, 64, 73, 76, 78, 82, 85, 100
bonds, 28, 39
budget resolution, 3, 34
businesses, 36, 47, 79, 84

C

candidates, vii, 1, 3
capital gains, 9, 22, 27, 28, 30, 43, 46, 58
cash, 5, 21, 22, 43, 44, 68, 75
categorization, 53
challenges, 21
charitable gifts, ix, 14, 22, 28, 32, 43, 44, 62, 68, 69, 70, 72, 76
charities, 18, 21, 38, 46, 57
Chief of Staff, 55
citizens, 35, 41
classes, vii, 1, 28, 31, 34, 40, 41, 42, 44, 58
classification, 84
classroom, 87
clothing, 45
color, iv
communities, 35, 36
community, 35, 36
compensation, 43, 90
complexity, x, 12, 13, 20, 21, 46, 77
compliance, xi, 5, 12, 16, 17, 38, 45, 46, 64, 78, 82, 84
complications, 46
computation, 46
computing, 46
Concise, 47
conflict, 9
Congress, iv, vii, xi, 1, 2, 11, 41, 48, 54, 56, 58, 61, 64, 71, 72, 78, 92, 98, 100
Congressional Budget Office, 9, 23, 25, 27, 55, 56
consensus, 10, 39, 53
conservation, 22, 27
consumption, 76

cost, 21, 22, 34, 36, 37, 75, 97
covering, 93
cumulative percentage, 40, 42
cure, 93

D

damages, iv
data analysis, 64, 73
deficit, 9, 64
depreciation, 37
depth, 57, 63, 73
disability, 43
disaster, 84, 96
distortions, 8, 72
distribution, vii, viii, 2, 8, 40, 47, 66, 69, 70, 73
diversity, 36
doctors, 54
donations, 21, 26, 38, 45
donors, 37
drugs, 93

E

earnings, viii, 2, 8, 10, 28, 37
economic consequences, 72
economic efficiency, vii, viii, 2, 3, 35, 36
economic growth, 34, 57
economics, 57
education, 57, 97
educational services, 39
egg, 35
energy, 43
equipment, 87, 98
equity, 5, 6, 11, 19, 37, 40, 45, 55, 94
evidence, 34, 57
exclusion, 5, 8, 15, 22, 36, 37, 56, 72, 75, 99
expenditures, vii, viii, ix, x, xi, 1, 2, 3, 4, 5, 6, 7, 8, 9, 12, 15, 16, 18, 19, 27, 28, 30, 33, 35, 40, 48, 53, 55, 62, 63, 70, 71, 72, 75, 77, 78, 79, 80, 84, 92, 98, 99
exposure, 36

F

fairness, 40
families, 36, 37
Federal Government, 26
financial, 36, 88, 97
flat-dollar, x, 12, 20, 39, 62, 73
formula, 23, 24, 25
foundations, 6, 96
fringe benefits, 3, 38
funds, 37, 38, 91

G

gambling, 6, 97
GAO, 53, 74
General Accounting Office, 53, 74
governments, 39
grants, 21, 38, 39
growth, 9, 36, 47, 57

H

health, 8, 15, 28, 41, 43, 45, 47, 54, 56, 58, 75, 87, 88, 89, 90
health care, 8, 58, 75, 88
health insurance, 15, 28, 43, 56, 75, 87, 88, 89, 90
heterogeneity, 31
history, 3, 56
home ownership, 11, 35
homeowners, 11, 13, 18, 19, 35, 37, 45, 57
homes, 19, 26, 28, 36, 37, 45
horizontal equity, 8, 11, 40, 45
House, 2, 53, 56
housing, viii, 2, 3, 11, 13, 31, 35, 36, 37, 47, 57

I

income distribution, 4, 14, 28, 32, 54, 73
individuals, vii, viii, ix, x, 1, 4, 7, 8, 11, 17, 18, 20, 22, 34, 35, 36, 37, 38, 42, 44, 46,

47, 61, 62, 63, 64, 65, 68, 72, 74, 75, 77, 78, 79, 84, 85, 87, 88, 92, 96, 98
inequality, 39
inflation, 20, 36, 47, 83, 84, 85, 89, 90, 100
injury, iv
insurance policy, 95
Internal Revenue Service, 13, 14, 29, 48, 49, 50, 51, 52, 54, 55, 56, 58, 59, 63, 65, 67, 68, 70, 71, 74, 81, 92, 98, 99, 100
investment, 6, 28, 54, 84, 95, 97, 100
IRC, 86, 87, 88, 89, 90, 91, 92, 93, 94, 95, 96, 97, 100
issues, 3, 8, 34, 37, 38, 40, 46, 54

J

job creation, 36, 73

L

labor market, 57
labor supply, viii, 2, 3, 9, 34
laws, 5, 72, 99
lead, ix, 9, 23, 32, 34, 36, 39, 45, 46, 61, 63, 64, 75
legislation, 5, 54
loans, 6, 19, 94
local government, x, 3, 6, 39, 77, 87
long-term care insurance, 75, 89, 93

M

magnitude, viii, 2, 36
majority, ix, 62, 66
management, 97
marginal tax bracket, x, 23, 56, 62, 74, 80
market failure, 36, 37
marriage, 83
married couples, 83, 85
materials, 87
matter, iv, 57
measurement, ix, 4, 53, 61, 63
medical, x, 3, 5, 7, 11, 12, 18, 19, 24, 35, 41, 43, 45, 48, 54, 55, 64, 69, 73, 75, 77, 81, 88, 90, 93, 100
medical care, 93
Medicare, 30, 41, 54, 57, 88
methodology, 44
Mexico, 55
middle class, 29
modifications, 46
museums, 38

N

negative effects, 14, 36
net investment, 95
neutral, viii, 2, 28, 34, 40, 44, 46

O

Office of Management and Budget, 53, 55, 75
officials, 87
OMB, 55

P

participants, 36, 90, 91
payroll, 43
pension plans, 9, 90
PEP, 53, 100
performing artists, 87
permission, iv
permit, viii, 2, 9, 29, 44
platform, 54
policy, vii, ix, 1, 2, 3, 14, 16, 21, 29, 31, 32, 33, 34, 39, 40, 48, 54, 61, 62, 63, 75, 76
policy options, ix, 16, 62, 63, 75
policymakers, viii, xi, 3, 7, 18, 36, 39, 61, 63, 78
population, 38, 39
portfolio, 36
positive externalities, 35, 36
poverty, 38
preparation, iv, 6, 7, 46, 97

present value, 9
President, vii, 1, 2, 15, 18, 24, 33, 46, 53, 55, 100
President Obama, 15, 33
presidential campaign, 54, 57, 73
prevention, 93
progressive income tax, 42
property taxes, ix, 5, 19, 20, 24, 37, 41, 42, 62, 68, 93, 94
proposition, 3
public goods, 39
public health, 37

R

rate of return, 75
real estate, ix, 5, 19, 20, 21, 22, 24, 36, 40, 42, 57, 62, 68, 72
real property, 27, 31, 37
recognition, 76
recommendations, iv
reform, vii, viii, ix, 1, 2, 3, 8, 9, 12, 38, 54, 57, 62, 63, 72, 73
Reform, 18, 19, 27, 42, 47, 53, 54, 55, 56, 57, 58, 74, 83, 99, 100
reforms, 19, 20, 45, 100
reintroduction, 86
rent, 36, 37
requirements, 78, 84, 88, 90
researchers, 15, 55, 76
Residential, 53, 56
resources, 11, 58
response, 17, 71, 74, 75
restrictions, 6, 8, 9, 11, 12, 15, 30, 34, 48, 56
retirement, 9, 22, 35, 43, 90, 91
rights, iv
risk, 36, 37
rules, viii, 2, 46, 84

S

savings, 3, 9, 10, 34, 43, 80, 87, 88, 90
savings account, 43, 87, 88
savings rate, 9
school, 87
scope, 79, 99
security, 43
self-employed, 28, 43, 88, 89, 90
self-employment, 28, 43, 89
Senate, 2, 27, 34, 54, 56, 58, 92, 98
services, iv, 11, 39, 87, 93
showing, 5
side effects, 3
simulation, 43
small businesses, 75
social benefits, 35
social policy, 11, 35
social security, 43
Social Security, 22, 41
social welfare, 82
society, 36
software, 46, 87, 97
SOI, 14, 29, 49, 50, 51, 52, 54, 56, 58, 59, 63, 65, 67, 68, 70, 71, 74
sole proprietor, 47, 84
solution, 47, 54
South Dakota, 54
spending, 5, 11, 37, 39, 45, 54, 100
SS, 86
state, vii, ix, x, 1, 3, 5, 6, 8, 10, 11, 13, 14, 19, 20, 24, 27, 28, 30, 31, 32, 39, 40, 41, 42, 43, 44, 45, 47, 48, 54, 56, 57, 58, 62, 66, 68, 69, 70, 72, 73, 75, 77, 81, 87, 93, 94
states, 20, 39, 54
statistics, 10, 21
structure, ix, x, 62, 66, 67, 72, 74, 93
structuring, 17, 18
subsidy, 35, 36, 39

T

target, viii, ix, 2, 3, 4, 19, 32, 34, 36, 62, 64, 73, 100
Task Force, 18, 55
tax base, 2, 3, 34, 47, 48
tax credits, xi, 15, 18, 20, 78, 79
tax data, 4, 64, 67

tax deduction, vii, viii, ix, x, xi, 1, 3, 5, 10, 12, 20, 24, 28, 30, 34, 36, 38, 39, 42, 44, 48, 53, 55, 56, 61, 62, 63, 64, 66, 67, 69, 72, 73, 74, 76, 77, 78, 79, 81, 86, 99, 100
tax incentive, 37, 75
tax increase, 32
tax policy, 3, 4, 8, 19, 33, 40, 54, 64
tax rates, xi, 2, 3, 8, 9, 10, 15, 17, 23, 25, 27, 28, 29, 30, 31, 32, 33, 34, 36, 38, 39, 40, 44, 47, 56, 57, 66, 76, 78, 79, 85
tax reform, viii, 2, 3, 9, 11, 12, 19, 22, 35, 39, 46
tax system, 15, 99
taxation, 8, 28, 73, 74, 78, 91
taxes, vii, ix, x, 1, 3, 5, 8, 9, 10, 11, 12, 14, 17, 18, 19, 20, 22, 24, 30, 31, 32, 33, 37, 39, 40, 42, 43, 45, 47, 48, 53, 54, 56, 57, 58, 61, 62, 63, 64, 66, 68, 69, 70, 72, 73, 74, 75, 77, 79, 80, 81, 85, 93, 94, 100
taxpayers, viii, 2, 3, 4, 5, 6, 9, 12, 13, 16, 17, 18, 19, 21, 29, 31, 39, 40, 42, 45, 46, 54, 58, 63, 65, 69, 75, 81, 82, 90, 91, 94, 95
tenure, 36
theft, 6, 7, 12, 54, 84, 96, 100
trade, viii, 2, 3, 32
trade-off, viii, 2, 3, 32
transaction costs, 57
transactions, 46, 97
transportation, 93, 97
treatment, 22, 44, 45, 46, 75, 79, 92, 93, 99
tuition, 92

U

universities, 38
urban, 76
Urban Institute, 53, 58, 76, 100

V

valuation, 22, 46
variations, 25
vehicles, 5, 20, 56
vertical equity, 8, 35, 40, 44

W

wages, 28, 43, 93
Washington, 53, 54, 56, 58, 71, 75, 92, 98, 99, 100
waste, 39
waste management, 39
welfare, 82
White House, 55
withdrawal, 43
workers, 41
working groups, 3
World War I, 47

Y

yield, 24